TWO-MILE OPEN WATER SWIM WITH HURDLES

By Martin Miller-Yianni

A SIX-MONTH JOURNEY FROM
NON-SWIMMER TO
2-MILE OPEN WATER SWIMMER

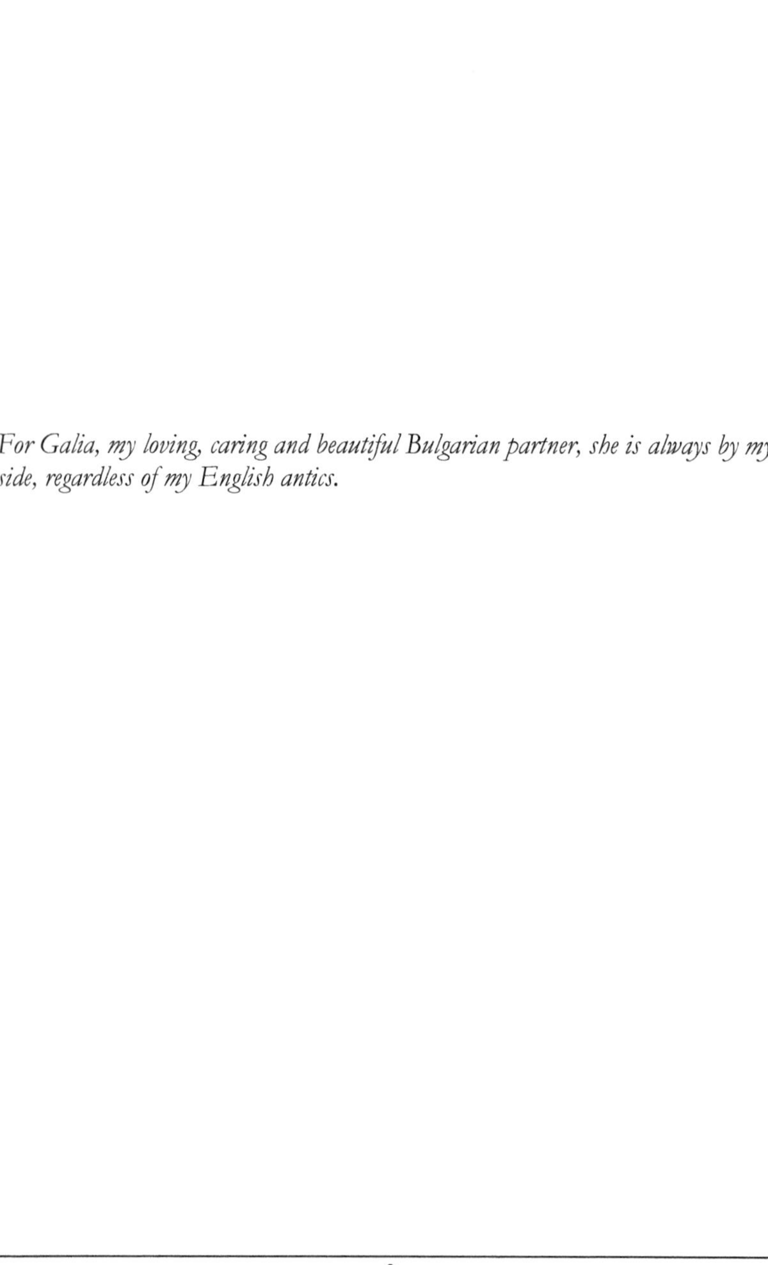

For Galia, my loving, caring and beautiful Bulgarian partner, she is always by my side, regardless of my English antics.

COPYRIGHT

Publisher: M P Miller-Yianni, Yambol, Bulgaria

Published (paperback) February 2020 (First Edition)

ISBN 978-619-91520-2-7

A catalogue record for this book is available from:

The National Register of Published Books in Bulgaria

bulevard "Vasil Levski" 88, 1504 Sofia, Bulgaria

ABOUT THE AUTHOR

Martin Miller-Yianni was born in Erith, England in 1958. When approaching 50 years of age, the former Primary classroom teacher decided to move away from his UK homeland and seek a new life. A simple, free and calm lifestyle returning to old values would have always remained a dream without that move.

A new life in foreign lands began in October 2005. He took on a smallholding enterprise in an outback village called Skalitsa some 37 kilometres south of the City of Yambol based in the southwest region of Bulgaria. Subsequently, he met his Bulgarian partner Galia in 2006.

The recently retired English expatriate now finds himself busier than ever managing a smallholding and living off the land. He started up a new farming project in another village closer to Yambol in the spring of 2019.

Having been immersed in Bulgarian life and culture, this inspired him to write books. To date, Martin has written and published a variety of books about life, history and culinary delights of Bulgaria. The writing continues here with the turn of a new and different water-based adventure.

FORWARD

Preparing, training and completing an endurance swimming challenge for the first time late in life isn't as easy as you think.

Despite not being able to swim having been scarred with a fear of water historically, the challenge went forward. Overcoming this phobia was the big first big step, but it didn't end there. The ultimate objective was to complete a two-mile open water swimming event in London's Serpentine Lake in Hyde Park some six months later. For a dedicated landlubber, this was a trial of courage, sacrifice and not least, foolishness in the eyes of many that surrounded him.

Living in outback Bulgaria, there was no other alternative other than to learn how to swim single-handedly with no support locally. Along with the self-taught program, many other hurdles turned this into a mission to avoid failure. One of the main challenges was trying to achieve this goal on a very tight budget equal to the economic and frugal Bulgarian lifestyle.

A simple task of finding a place to swim shouldn't pose any problems to most; even perhaps taken for granted. Finding places to swim in was not the case in south-eastern Bulgaria. As it turned out, a grace of good fortune was needed to straddle this particular hurdle and thus avoid cancelling the whole concept.

Trying to overcome and deal with the fear of water was a gradual process and was not noticeable on a day to day basis. This fear still exists, even during the successful completion of the 2-mile open water event, which was not without moments of panic, anxiety and fear. Learning how to deal with these traumatic moments was the key over the six months of training.

Taking steps towards overcoming phobias is difficult but not impossible. It clears the way for other goals beyond those fears that can, in turn, make a dream become a reality.

- Hopefully, others will gain inspiration from this story -

List of Contents

Chapter 1

The Swimming Challenge Concept

Life is littered with goals and challenges, yet some are made just for the hell of it. Many people go through their lives with a never-ending quest for extending themselves. Perhaps this is something that occurs in the build-up of genes we have. There is this compulsive adrenaline rush for pushing yourself to achieve more. I shudder at the thought of resigning myself into fading away into the realms of elderly oblivion. Is this the consequence of a fear of ageing or being labelled or seen as old?

There is a spirit inside me that won't believe or accept that a life of 60 years in this world has already passed. With this, the idea of a 2-mile swim for a non-swimmer, (that's me) was perhaps to prove this point.

Having completed the Surrey 100-mile bike ride in 2016, I registered to take part in the event again in 2018. I knew full well I wouldn't be able to take part due to costs but mainly the complicated logistics involved as I was now living in Bulgaria. In the back of my mind; however, there was something in my head saying, 'You never know.'

When I was accepted, there was an option given to put it off for the following year if competitors couldn't compete for whatever reason. So with hope hanging on, that's what I did. An offer to take part in the 2019 ride duly came about, but nothing had changed about me not being able to compete and I now had reluctantly resigned myself to forget about the idea.

With an email message from London Marathon Ltd asking me to pay a £96 fee for the 2019 cycle event, I knew yet again the cost of flying with a bicycle and the expense of accommodation was well beyond my means. Even higher costs with the event taking place in August, the peak holiday time with traditional criminal hiked travel prices. Just the basics of me travelling alone would amount to well over £500 and doubled if Galia came with me. I was frustrated but had to resign myself yet again, not being able to take part.

Notwithstanding, contained within the message was a section referring to competitors who had completed three London Endurance Sporting Challenges. These competitors would be entitled to another medal and would also qualify for entry into the London Classics Hall of Fame. I read on with interest.

Having completed the London Marathon way back in 1982 and now with the Surrey 100 bike ride in the bag, I was two-thirds of the way there. Provoked thoughts invaded my mind going for the missing third event, which was to complete a 2-mile swim in the open waters of the Serpentine Lake in London's Hyde Park. This event was due to take place in September 2019.

The thought of taking up another endurance sporting challenge when I will have arrived at the age of 61 years old filled me with uncontained excitement. The quest from what I gathered at this point looked demanding but undoubtedly feasible. On consulting Galia about this, she was okay with the idea if that's what I wanted.

Yet again, here I am with another challenge in front of me. It was a great feeling knowing that there was now something to work towards and looked forward to planning and starting up training in earnest.

There was this fixation thinking that the swimming event would be more comfortable than the Marathon and Cycle Ride. Both the Marathon and Cycling events went on for well over four hours, exhausting and demanding but enjoyable. I predicted that the swim should only last about two to three hours. Not having the skill of being able to swim at this stage was the reason. I could float on water and drift forward with a slow and laboured breaststroke come doggy-paddle style, but that wasn't swimming, just slightly faster than treading water. However, with a bit of time training learning how to swim and a programme to build up stamina, what's the problem?

The 2019 Swim Serpentine Emblem

There was a little wait to apply for the event, which was due at the beginning of February, so my training plans were on hold until then.

Nothing is Easy

True to form February arrived and a window for applications for the 2-mile swimming event in Hyde Park opened. There was no hesitation in me applying. There were options for different starting times. I chose the earliest 2-mile group starting at 09:35, so I would finish before midday

All the online application processes completed, which brought me now to the point of paying. It then transpired that all of my three bank cards were blocked. At this point, I had no idea why or what problems lay ahead.

After contacting my bank, they confirmed that they had removed all blocks and the payment should now go through. It was now a few days later and a fear that my request for that 09:35 start, which was probably the most popular, would soon be filled. To my dismay payment still wasn't being authorised despite the bank's assurances. Time was rolling on and more frustration setting in with the growing fear of missing out on the completion of my application.

The London Marathon helpline was the next step with an email inquiring whether there was an option of another method of payment. There was more worry with the reply received telling me that there was no other way of paying. It had to be done online with the current unwavering system in place. The helpline asked me to check that all numbers, names and dates were accurate; as if I wouldn't have checked this anyway!

With time ticking away the event organisers now suggested I get someone in the UK to pay on my behalf. I asked my son Nathan in the UK to help and he was most obliging. However, even more disappointment and frustration followed when we found that his bank card was also blocked. It was now the turn of his mother, my ex-wife to try with her card. It ended up with the same result; authorisation refused yet again. By this time, I was quite discouraged with the total ridiculousness of the situation.

The next step was to feed all these problems back to the event helpline. They now suggested I call them up on the phone and they will try to pay with my card online from their end. I wasn't happy, even annoyed by this suggestion. The cost of international phone calls is extortionate on my mobile phone. Added to the build-up of annoyance was the London Marathon helpline staff not being allowed to make overseas calls. With this mandatory rule in place, they came up with the idea of my son in the UK ringing them up with my bank card details. On the face of it, it would be cheaper on phone bills, but this to my mind was not a good idea. Giving out my bank credit card details to my son was not an issue, but then for him to hand this information over to another party was far too risky in my eyes.

Desperation now kicked in and it was back to the bank again after nearly a week from their initial investigations. They now insisted that everything was in order their end and there was nothing more they could do.

I was now almost resigned to giving up with no other sensible means of being able to pay despite the efforts made over two frustrating weeks. I went to bed that evening depressed and didn't get much sleep that night for what I deemed as discrimination for oversea applicants.

After more thought, I decided to throw caution to the wind and ring the event helpline. I knew that giving third parties my bank details was risky, but there was no other way to pay. I also was fully aware that payment would be blocked from their end as the payment process is the same as before with me, my son and my ex-wife.

I went ahead and called up the UK London Marathon Helpline with low expectations. Much to my dismay, an automated voice and extended menus came about. Why wasn't I surprised? It was a full three minutes going through that mad maze before I got cut off! With more frustration, I called again and a repeat of the problem getting cut off. It was now back to the helpline via an email and another day passes before I get a reply. Another day ticks on by every time I contact them this way.

A reply was received the next day as expected. They gave instructions when using the automated telephone system, namely, to wait for the menu at the end of the computerised talk. Then choose the 'swim' option. I felt irate as it was like taking a step back in the process and besides, mounting telephone costs each time. Nevertheless, it was back on the phone, apprehensive and angry of the mounting bills that 'tick-tocked' away in time. Trying to get through to a human on the helpline was a frustrating hair-pulling experience. This anger and frustration continued throughout this process, knowing that is was doomed to fail.

Finally, after many minutes on the automated menu, I got through to a person on the helpline. This person was called Ellie and was the same person who I had been communicating for over two weeks via email. We went through the process and guess what? It failed! There was further waiting and minutes were mounting up while Ellie consulted the event accountant, who may have an answer. The idea that came back was to use my bank account taking the fee of £54 on a manual payment system which they could organise in their office.

So now being resigned to this idea, my bank details were given again over the phone. There was a promise to shred all my bank details once the payment had gone through. I asked Ellie to confirm by email when completed as I didn't want to hold on for added phone bills costs − 15 minutes had now passed. She agreed to email me later in the day to confirm matters.

The calls cost over 22 leva leaving me with a sense of guilt and frustration. There is a reason or these emotions as living here in Bulgaria with a very modest budget causes financial concerns for us when these things happen. Economic issues hit hard when the high costs cast a vindictive element to overseas applications. Knowing the entry fee of £54 was one thing, we accept that, but unnecessary added expenses such as the phone calls are hard to come to terms.

No email arrived later in the day to confirm my entry, so there was more worry built up that evening and throughout the night. The fact they had open access to my bank details was perhaps the highest on the list of concerns.

Another day on and an email was finally received confirming payment of £54 taken from my bank account. My bank details were also confirmed as having been shredded by Ellie. A unique voucher code was issued as I had to apply online again and use that to gain entry into the process. There was an expiry date on the voucher of three days, but there was no chance of missing that deadline as I applied straight away. There was a hanging belief that gaining entry and being accepted for this event may now actually happen.

Fears allayed, not only did I gain entry, but they granted the 09:35 start I wanted. From the nerves of frustration, a new set of nerves were now taking over. The focus now was on the 2-mile swimming challenge and competing in the event six months later in September.

I emailed Ellie thanking her for the support promising to try and see her at the event to thank her again personally. She confirmed she'd be there, but she didn't know in what capacity and hoped I would enjoy the occasion.

With the 2-mile swim in open water challenge now in front of me, it just remains for me to find some water to practice. There was only one outdoor swimming pool on a holiday complex in a village some 15 kilometres from Yambol. Other than that it would be a drive for an hour to reach hotel resorts on the Black Sea and in other big cities. There were no other venues to practice swimming other than local reservoirs, rivers and lakes. These open water options would be far too cold right now leading up to June but may be useful beyond that month.

There is always the Black Sea during spring and early summer, but due to the distance, it would have to be sporadic visits maybe once each month. However, it could still be built into the training process later on. The problem was where to swim from February until then.

Before I even conceived of the idea of swimming 2-miles, I knew there was a swimming pool in my home town of Yambol. It was in a high school, but I had never used it as I thought it was only for students. Galia has a cousin I sometimes go out cycling with and told him about the idea of a long swim in open water in London. On asking whether he'd be interested in doing this with me, he revealed that he is a very competent swimmer. He suggested we should use the Yambol school swimming pool together sometime, but due to his commitments as a Doctor, he couldn't go to London for the event with me. It was then that it dawned that the school pool was open to the public and not just students. The local school pool now opened the door fully to having a place to train on my doorstep. How lucky was that?

It was now Friday 22nd February and a trip was made to the high school to make inquiries about using the pool. The local pool was now very much an essential part of the training plan and without it a non-event. The opening times were Monday to Friday with 10:00 starts through to 18:00 with an hour break for lunch. The fees for students was 1.50 leva and non-students 3 leva for a 1-hour session.

Inside the complex, there were changing rooms, showers and toilets as you would expect. There was also a lifeguard on duty full-time and lots of swimming aids such as floats, flippers and hand paddles etc. Most public pools are 25 metres in length; this one was 17 metres. Given the benefit of having a pool and only a 10-minute walk from our apartment was enough. Another bonus was the heated water at a very comfortable temperature of 27C.

Swimming caps were compulsory, so it was off to a local shop to find one. Also to look for a pair of goggles to avoid red eyes from chlorine after each session. We found a cap for 3 leva with 'BULGARIA' printed on it alongside the national flag. There was also a pair of cheap swimming goggles that came with earplugs and nose clamp for 2 leva. The total cost of these items was only 5 leva. Naturally, I have my doubts on how efficient they would be with a rock bottom price and subsequent commensurate quality. We'll see.

I decided to start training the following Monday 25th February. In the intervening weekend, there were lots of researching for swimming tips on techniques in preparation for open water swims. It was at this time I realised that the challenge was not going to be as easy as I envisaged. The event is not a race with my mindset on just taking it slow and relaxed, even if it takes all morning to complete the distance.

There is a mandatory requirement using a tow float in the event swim and possibly a wetsuit if the water temperature is below 15C. The tow float would be something to use as a resting tool and of course another additional cost to be taken on board. There are cheap Chinese made tow floats knocking around on eBay for about £5, but with the reviews seen, there are safety issues. More durable makes are around £20-25. The realised costs of swimming equipment are all adding up and going well beyond the original budget for the event.

A wetsuit is an even bigger issue for me from the point of cost. I can't afford to buy one and just to hire one for the day is around £40! If it becomes compulsory on the day and we would know a couple of weeks before the event, this would be something of a problem. This issue would have to be worked out later in the year - early days.

The 3 leva Swimming Cap

Flights to London from Bulgaria in September were sourced and found. Sofia to Stansted was the only viable option, unfortunately having to fly with Ryanair. Not a fan of that airline at all, but no choice in the matter with minimal funds. The cost was £85 for a return flight.

The plan now was to arrive in the UK on the 20th September, have a one night stay in London. Compete in the swimming event on the 21st and leave the UK at 06:30 on Sunday 22nd. There will be no sleep at all that last night to save on the costs of another night in London. I envisaged sleeping on a bench in the

Marble Arch area until late, then pottering about in Stansted Airport for 5-6 hours in the early hours of Sunday morning.

Transfers by coach from Stansted to London were £17 return and a hotel room only two kilometres from Hyde Park costing £35. There were hostel options, but I couldn't face sharing a bathroom with anyone; this was one luxury I won't sacrifice. Back in Bulgaria, the fare from my home in Yambol to Sofia Airport return was another 50 leva.

The total cost without a wetsuit is now around £250, which spread over six months is affordable. There was an ongoing 6 to 9 leva each week for two or three visits to the pool. A nominal saving by using the school showers and not at home is a bonus. Yes, we think that way all the time and have to if you have read past writings of our frugal life in Bulgaria. We decided right from the start that I will travel alone solely down to the cost. No issues being on my own, in fact, less stressful with me worrying about Galia while I'm in the water for hours on end.

Everything now set up and ready to start training and thrilled with that prospect.

Chapter 2 (March)

The First Training Session

There are no crowds in the swimming pool in the mornings; this was something of a relief to hear. So my alarm was set for 07:30 on this cold Monday morning. Adrenalin was running high with the thought of starting training in earnest. Breakfast was made up of muesli and a sliced banana alongside a hot refreshing mint tea to wash it down. My morning routine remained the same with one hour of piano practice (fitness for fingers). This routine is perfect as it gave time for my breakfast to digest. I could see this plan continuing.

Starting up swimming on top of existing and ongoing sporting activities, namely jogging, cycling and gym work looked intense and demanding. Was there a triathlete in the making now or will something have to drop? Not at this stage although I had been advised by many people not to overdo things at my age. But then most of the advice was coming from a sedate band of inactive beer-loving Bulgarian smokers!

The Mathematics High School, 'Atanas Radev' Yambol

Meanwhile, having arrived at the high school complex, there was a walk across the students play area to reach and enter the swimming pool block. The fee of

3 leva paid-up to a middle-aged woman operating the minute cash desk cubical. She didn't hesitate to ask me whether I had a swimming cap. With a nod from me, she duly got out of her cubical and showed me where the changing rooms, shower, toilets and pool were respectively. She knew it was my first time here.

The changing rooms had a multi-rowed set of wooden lockers at the far end, but they were all ajar seemingly with every lock broken. I did wonder whether anyone had stuff stolen when seeing this. It was, therefore, natural to be a little nervous and apprehensive about leaving my wallet and mobile phone there. I wrapped them up in a plastic bag and took them to the pool with me feeling somewhat self-conscious about doing this. There was another set of clothing hung up on a peg with shoes and bag on the floor, so I knew I wasn't going to be alone in the pool.

Trying on the swimming cap was distinctly alien to me having never worn one before. It was like putting a condom on your head and felt uncomfortable and claustrophobic - no doubt I'd get used to it eventually. With my goggles now on and in place, this just compounded the sense of claustrophobia. The feeling of being trapped was something I wasn't relaxed with at all. It was off to the pool regardless of these discerning issues.

On entering the pool area, there was indeed one elderly swimmer in the water going up and down the pool using a variety of strokes each length. More interestingly, there was also a young female lifeguard on duty. Most of the time, she was engaged in conversation with a dressed young man, but I'm sure she would rescue me if I got into difficulties despite the male distraction. The swimming session was the start of something I thought I might enjoy, but that positive expectation didn't last long.

When I was young, it took ages for me to build up the confidence to put my head underwater with an inherent fear of deep water. Then in my teenage years, there was the time in London's Hampstead Heath ponds, where I nearly drowned trying to save a friend who was distressed in the water. On my approach, his panic pushed me under where I inhaled water into my lungs. It was very close to drowning with some respiration needed to expel the water. I distinctly remember being sick expelling dirty pond water. These moments return as flashbacks whenever I am in the water near people triggering a great sense of anxiety and panic.

On vacation in locations which had pools or the sea to swim, I could manage a clumsy breaststroke/doggy paddle style for a few metres with a recovery session by floating on my back. On the odd occasion, I attempted a few metres of the front crawl with a high head position well above the water. This style of swimming could only be sustained at most up to around 15 metres.

Running out of breath, exhaustion leading to panic due to trying to maintain a high head position was the reason. Now I do consider myself to be fit but could never understand why I get into a state of exhaustion only after a short time swimming front crawl.

Back in the high school pool, I started with a couple of sluggish lengths of breaststroke used as a warm-up session. By the end of this short distance, I desperately needed a rest after being completely exhausted. It took a few minutes to recover.

After the recovery, I tried the front crawl and couldn't even manage a length. There was a combination of exhaustion and panic leading up to the inevitable halt. Not being able to breathe while swimming was a big issue here and from that point, my feet were on the floor to recover my breath. This sense of suffocating was worrying, given the 2-mile distance needed in September. Also more worrying that it would be in deep open waters amongst crowds of other swimmers. My thoughts at that moment were, 'what the hell have I let myself into here?' All the payments made for the event including flights and hotel fees are all non-refundable. I just couldn't give up from the investment made let alone the dent that would hangover into my pride and ego. My only salvation here was this was the first day and it couldn't possibly get worse on the next outing.

I finished the session with a few clumsy breaststroke lengths with lots of intermittent breaks. There was no return to the front crawl style as I knew that my confidence would sink even lower if I did. After only 25 minutes in the water, I decided to shower and go home with a hypothetic tail between my legs. While recovering my breath, I watched a couple of other swimmers who had joined us in the pool. They glided along in a speedy front crawl fashion as if there was no effort to it at all and without any breaks length after length. How do they do that? How can I replicate their style? Can I overcome this return of the fear of deep water and panic not being able to breathe? Lots of questions without any answers on this first day. For sure it seems that this will now become a more significant challenge than the 26-mile marathon or 100-mile bike ride on good old terra firma.

In the Pool for More

It had been two days of deep thought and reflection after the shock of the first training session. Time was spent surveying tips from swimming experts online. Surely things would improve on the second swimming session. There was no other way to think right now, other than being positive.

The same routine was taken to the pool today. The same swimmer as on Monday had yet again beaten me into the pool. While I was changing a young man came in to change room and told me that the lady cashier wanted to see me before as I had short-changed her by 30 stotinki. Fee issues had to be sorted on my way out after the swim as I had my swimming trunks on and ready to swim. I duly made my way to the pool for the start of another session, albeit with 30 stotinki on my mind throughout today's swimming routine.

A different lifeguard was on duty today and she was much more in attendance and observant to happenings in the pool than the lady on Monday. This lifeguard was without a young male distraction. Mind you, Monday's lifeguard was much prettier!

The swimming cap and goggles again were giving me some concerns. I just couldn't get away from the sense of claustrophobia and the feeling today was worse than Monday as the googles now seeped water and steamed up. Why the seeping water didn't happen on Monday was a mystery, but the reason for steaming up was evident. My online research came up with the suggestion of wiping a bit of washing-up liquid inside the googles to prevent steamed up. Smearing worked on Monday, but I didn't prepare this today. The water seepage is more of an issue as the only solution to the problem was to stop and empty them, giving me grief each time.

Nervousness suddenly came over me when I first tried to do a simple breaststroke. A panic set in before completing the end of the first length and I had to stop. The thought of putting my head underwater now had become a severe issue; I just couldn't bring myself to do it. Submerging my head was worse than Monday and I don't know why. Before, in many spa centre pools and sea waters, my head underwater was not an issue. Where do I go now with this new plague of fear?

Another tip I picked up online the day before was just a simple exercise of dipping your head underwater, expelling air while submerged then rising out of the water and inhale. Five minutes of this simple exercise brought about a more relaxed state, in fact, so much so that I now dared myself to try the front crawl again.

The effort lasted nearly a whole length, albeit with panic breathing every two strokes on the left. Left side breathing felt more comfortable than the right, maybe because of my dominant left-handedness. There were many failings here, but the main issue was having to come to a grinding halt with feet firmly on the pool floor. The cause of this was directly related to the build-up of anxiety. Before too long, I was entirely out of breath and exhausted. It was a terrible feeling of helplessness not having a facility or technique with this stroke style. My vision of future training sessions was drastically different from what I initially thought. I realized now that the objective had to be focused entirely on learning how to swim.

The training programmes initially based on endurance and stamina would have to wait a while. The smaller goal now is to master at least a length of the pool in front crawl without baling out from panic attacks with feet grounded.

The session finished with a couple more breaststroke lengths. The aim was to try and relax and avoid moments of anxiety. Despite the efforts, this didn't work with my mind primarily fixed on the bad experiences earlier. Looking ahead I again wondered with trepidation on how I would cope in deep water and with crowded swimmers let alone the 2-mile distance required with the event.

The Mathematics High School Swimming Pool

A 30 minutes programme today and to be quite frank worse than the previous session on Monday. Due to an increased fear of inhaling water with no breathing technique caused panic, this was indeed a demoralising session. Working on these issues is needed before any other form of training plans can continue. A coach or trainer would be beneficial, but for the meantime, it will have to be solely free online coaches from afar. There is a little trickle of reassurance from time factors here as this was only the second session and there are a full six months to prepare for the event. I also think that diagnosing what the problems are was a good starting point. Giving up isn't one of the options despite the big step back in confidence since starting training. I paid the 30 stotinki owed on my way out with an apology and with that off my mind I felt a little better.

A Bit More Constructive

My mind was full of masterful plans to conquer the issues of breathing and panic caused by water intake. In this first week of training, which had been quite traumatic to date, taking advice online from swimming experts was my only option without any first-hand support. Information had been thoroughly researched online over the last few days. All the help seen were variations on the same theme, namely to stay relaxed and calm, work on correct posture and practice the timing of inhaling and exhaling. These were all part of moving progress forward trying to solve the problems from technical issues found; all of which common with learner swimmers.

The time was ripe to forget about getting more lengths of swimming until I had learned how to swim; otherwise, it was just sessions of practising bad habits. It was funny how I thought I could swim before now. Staying afloat is easy, making painfully slow headway using bad swimming technique is just unsustainably and foolhardy over a 2-mile distance so this had to change.

It was an extended weekend of celebratory holidays in Bulgaria starting with the 1st March being Baba Marta Den, (Grandmother Martha Day) which was also my name day. These celebrations carried on through to Monday 4th March where there was another National holiday dedicated to the Liberation of Bulgaria from the Ottoman rule on the 3rd March.

Because of the public holidays, I called at the pool to ask whether they were open on Friday and subsequent Monday as I planned to train on those days. Friday they were free, but Monday closed so already there was a break in the proposed training schedule. No matter, Tuesday will be just as good. I'm not at all exhausted after each session right now, so two days in a row won't do any harm with just practising technique with no stamina work involved.

It was with a fresh mind while walking the short distance to the pool today. The thoughts on the bad experiences of the last two sessions were made easier on me by merely thinking I was trying to run before I can walk.

Goggles duly smeared with washing up liquid this time, so no fear of steaming up as I'm sure that's why they did last Wednesday. I got there 15 minutes before it officially opened at 10:00, but had to wait a while until the cashier had done her accounts on her little retro electronic cash register. The long list of accounts came streaming out of the machine eventually, which was a sure sign that she had finished. While waiting, three other non-student swimmers turned up. This little crowd was the most people I'd seen here to date in the morning. My sole thought was on how many swimmers and how many swimming lanes there were? Would I have to share? Would this be an indignant gesture because of my stop-go swimming style where I would hold up other swimmers sharing the lane? Everyone else I had seen swimming in the pool so far was competent and smooth operational swimmers. I was probably fitter than all of them, but not at all obvious in the pool with my distinct lack of swimming technique. I was clear that I wasn't anywhere near the swim fit category like others pool attendees had reached - yet.

I had read that many runners and cyclists who are super fit just cannot hack swimming and have the same symptoms as I am experiencing. Not being able to complete a length without having to stop was a common problem for beginners from what I've read up. That made me feel more comfortable knowing that I could solve this over time with perseverance. But this can only be done with a strict 'back to basics' working on the methods recommended by swimming experts online.

Online advice on board and it was into the water and a five-minute session of a drill called 'bobbing'. Bobbing is standing in shallow water, taking a deep breath through the mouth and then ducking under the water to blowing out air through the nose. It is then a simple process of repeating this sequence robotically many times. It was quite easy, although for some reason there were times I sensed a prelude to panic. The thought that I might inhale underwater was the reason. Why would I think this? Why would I do that? There wasn't any logic for those thoughts.

Simple as the drill is, there were a few occasions where I exhaled the air out too fast. With this, I had to hold my breath a little before being able to inhale once above water again. I guessed it was good to practice as it trains you to be able to have more control the volume of air expelled. The five-minute bobbing exercise was done three times during this session. It didn't feel like I had this mastered by any means. However, it was only the first session of this exercise today. Still, more practice and focusing on the control of the air is needed to avoid a gasping action when coming up for air. Future sessions should sort this out. The more I do this drill, the more automated it should become and therefore, less thinking about the silly 'what if?' scenarios.

The next routine was just to get some front crawl strokes. The aim was to have the head face down in the water while holding your breath throughout. Then pushing off with both hands straight out in front with the body straight and paralleled float on top of the water. As simple as that!

It felt like everything was done in slow motion while holding your breath and gliding forward. Once moving off with a relaxed leg kick, each arm, in turn, does a complete stroke cycle. Then bring the arm back to where it starts parallel with the other arm. Only then does the opposite arm begin to complete a stroke cycle and so on…. After six strokes, (three with each arm), you stop, breath, recover and repeat. I practised this many times, which caused me to feel relaxed and very comfortable with this sequence with the arm actions. There was, of course, no breathing involved here, just a focus on smooth, slow, economical strokes and straight body without any panic. With the head underwater facing the bottom of the pool, this creates minimum drag. Repeating this again and again and turned out to be something I ended up enjoying. There was always an end in sight to breathing each time. It was strange having to wait for each arm to arrive before the other one starts and there was still a tendency to start one arm before the other comes over. Doing this correctly and naturally will happen with more sessions.

The last bit of training advice taken up from online sources was tackling the area of breathing techniques for front crawl. Luckily this school swimming pool had lots of swimming aids including a simple kickboard. I hold the kickboard with both hands stretched out in front with a relaxed leg kick to get you going. Again with both hands on the float, the head is submerged facing the bottom of the pool. I had found that I am more comfortable breathing in from my left side. With this left preference, the exercise, for now, is just for my left arm stroke and inhaling from that same side and then releasing my left arm to do a complete stroke and back to holding the kickboard again. As the left-hand leaves the float going into the stroke, the body naturally swivels/twists clockwise to the left. When the head turns left, I take in air the mouth. With the kickboard back in both hands, a gentle exhaling of air through the nose. My head now faces down underwater. As the left arm stroke returns another inhale it taken on the left side wake.

As I practised, it became more comfortable and I could now complete lengths quite easily without getting too exhausted. It was a very pleasing achievement, given failings of the past two sessions. I felt a little corner turned with this exercise. There was a slight hiccup when I tried to do exercise this with the right side failing having swallowed water and had to stop feet landing on both occasions. I will continue now solely with the left to gain more confidence before trying that right side again!

With a little confidence instilled, I tried to go for a front crawl length without aids. It all started well, but by the time I had got halfway down the stretch, panic struck with water getting into my nose. All the bad habits returned with the return of anxiety as a consequence. It resulted in either continuing with a panic swim to the end of the length totally exhausted or just stopping with feet down on the floor. It was an unfortunate end to what I thought was something that started in a promising fashion.

School Pool Swimming Aids

The session had finished with two lengths of head-high, snail-paced breaststroke and in all honesty, was a bit of a relief. Then suddenly I found that I had been in the pool for 50 minutes. This session was 20 minutes longer than both previous sessions and more constructive.

I still can't believe how lucky I am to have a pool so close to home. Without this, taking part in the event in September just would not be possible. There is much work ahead in this pool into getting up and running with a simple front crawl action like all the other swimmers I had seen.

The next session is now due on Tuesday, 5th March. I was looking forward to doing the same things practised today, but with more confidence.

I saw a news article this morning about a Syrian refugee who nearly drowned trying to get to the UK crossing the sea. This man, who couldn't swim just one year ago is now in full training to compete in the 2020 Olympics as a swimmer; Such an inspirational story for anyone who wants to start learning to swim from scratch.

Sick and Disappointed

We were babysitting for five days over the Bulgarian National Holiday Weekend with Galia's sick, (as in not well) 2-year-old Grandson. We both got infected with a virus he was carrying. The suffering started and continued with sore throats, blocked sinuses, annoying coughing and headaches. The child is now back with his Mum and Dad, God bless him, after leaving the trail of illness behind him.

This weekend brought about a quest. The quest was to conduct full research online finding various swimming maestros who had published advice on swimming breathing techniques. They all make it look so easy. There was no online advice on how to overcome the triggering of panic attacks when water is accidentally taken in through the nose or mouth.

Thinking back to trips to the Black Sea and swimming in the sea, I remember it being much more relaxed there, even with being surrounded by crashing waves. I wondered why. I didn't seem to have any issues with my breaststroke with my head ducking underwater briefly then coming up for a breath every third stroke. I distinctly remember swimming a paddle style breaststroke moving slowly parallel to shore last summer. It was seemingly sustainable for a short period without getting too exhausted with slow, progressive tiredness. Somehow this could not be replicated in the swimming pool. It must be the saltwater causing my body to be become more buoyant, therefore resulting in a higher body and head position in the water. It wouldn't be wrong to assume with this, swimming in a pool or unsalted open water needs more energy than swimming in the sea. (That is taking out the equation of rough seas and strong currents.) This assumption didn't invoke more confidence seeing that the pool is my only swimming venue open to me right now.

An idea was found online with the use a snorkel; many swimmers use it in training. It was surprising to see that it is also allowed and used in swimming events. I understand that some swimmers with mobility issues which prevents them from turning their head to the side have no other option other than to use this aid in front crawl. A snorkel is a great ploy to use if issues of normal breathing remain unsolved. Therefore, this may be considered in due course if nothing improves in this area. It could lead to being the saviour of not having to give up because of lack of breathing technique. This idea is therefore viable, so why not give it a go if my problems with breathing persist?

Having joined up with an online sports social website called RealBuzz, I got advice from some very kind people on this site. They commented on my blog and tried to address the issues that I raised. The information given was to work hard on the breathing technique, then everything else would fall into place. The other tip was to invest in a coach who would undoubtedly put the method on the right track. I don't know why I tinkered with the idea of finding one as I knew this wouldn't happen. The reason was due mainly to the lack of swimming facilities and support here in Yambol, which was evident from day one. Facilities provided here are all geared up for children and students naturally. Also, being highly strung and a stubborn fool, any trainer, would have a headache taking me on.

The pool was closed yesterday due to the National holiday, as mentioned before. The plan still stood to get a session in today. I, therefore, set the alarm for 07:00, despite feeling having a rough night of illness from the virus that we were still suffering.

Obeying the alarm call this morning it was up straight away for the day ahead. The morning's order was two paracetamol, a light breakfast, one hour piano practise and then off to the pool. By the time I got to the school pool, I wasn't feeling too bright, even after medication carrying a stuffed up nose and heavy head.

The pool was empty but for the female lifeguard. It was on with the swim cap and goggles, but then eye-pieces decided to become pieces and fall apart. It took a few minutes to fathom out how to reassemble them. Being the cheapest set of goggles in the world at just the equivalent of around £1.30 it didn't surprise me this happened. I managed a bodge job with a big double knot on the elastic strap. Slipping out of place and falling apart again should now stop. I will have to google for goggles to search for another pair online.

I felt like I had a hangover with illness, but the plan was to go ahead and just work on the breathing and relaxing again, similar to the previous session. It had only been three days since the last session but felt like it had been ages. I did the therapeutic bobbing exercises for five minutes with better control with the exhaling. Then, in a more relaxed state, it was one length of breaststroke using shorter strokes and straighter leg kicks. Just as seen on a video online over the weekend I copied. It didn't make much difference to the speed of the swim, much to my disappointment. The shorter strokes meant it was harder to force my head up for breathing. There was now more chance of water up the nose and mouth and panic set in again. Despite this, I will persevere. I'm sure the issues of panic stems from the fear of inhaling water as every time that happens, my swim comes to an immediate halt.

It was now the turn of the kickboard aid moving with just a left-arm front crawl stroke and breathing only on the left side. Again, the slightest hint of water up the nose and my feet swiftly reached for the floor; this happened frequently. Surely other swimmers must have the same issues with the slightest splash causing water forced into my nasal. Nothing on the web to guide beginner swimmers on how to deal with that situation other than saying stay relax and don't panic. I can relax and avoid panicking when it doesn't happen but can't if it does! When water gets up my nose the feeling of being choked and suffocating happens hence the panic. How can you not panic with this happening? Stopping to expel water it is my only answer to dispel panic situations right now. How can this be resolved in another way while in swimming mode? There was no solution in my head right now.

Finishing the session with a slow breaststroke for two lengths, I left the water in a somewhat defeatist mood after only 40 minutes. Fifteen of those minutes was with my feet on the ground in the pool, getting my breath back or recovering from panic situations. Not to be put off with this I will try again tomorrow.

When showering a conversation took place another swimmer who I'd befriended. He was about the same age as me and swam twice a week just for fitness before going to work. He said that this is the only swimming pool locally, which just confirmed my suspicions that was the case after my extensive investigations. However, the information given was doubted later in the day.

A quick espresso coffee from a vending machine and in vain, I started looking for a swimming trainer online once arriving back home. There was some excitement seeing a website that said there were two swimming pools in Yambol. The first was the in the school I already use, which states for students only, but as I know, that is not the case. The other was a 25-metre Olympic standard pool with two female swimming coaches in another school complex. It went on to say that it was open all year round and was free to use. Why didn't I see this before? Why didn't anyone tell me about this that knew about my challenge? It was only some three kilometres from our apartment and of course, we made a beeline straight to the location.

We entered the big block building where the pool was situated. We thought it was strange seeing that only a single pedal bike chained up to a railing in an empty car park. There were two people in attendance at the little reception area which was just simple small cubical with a glass façade. We asked about the swimming pool and they told us that it wasn't working. They went on to say that there hadn't had been any water in it for over 15 years! We were 'gobsmacked'! What a let-down this was after such joy and excitement of the find on the website. The site strangely was up to date with all current swimming events and news.

It was retail therapy next after this quick rise of excitement and immediate disappointment. A supermarket was right next to this dysfunctional pool as we treated ourselves to ice cream. This treat was enjoyed immensely on this hot and sunny day. The only option of a place to swim remains as it was, namely the mathematics high school.

Still feeling unwell in the afternoon and even worse in the evening, my thoughts were that it wouldn't be wise for another swimming session tomorrow. My stubbornness may win and I will probably still go. It is just like being forced to go to work in the UK even when sick.

Back on Track

It had been a week of being bedridden and flu was the reason. There was no way I could have gone swimming on any of the days of last week with the heavy cough, aching head and blocked sinuses. There was always that dare to go and train regardless of health issues, but this time there was a little thought before diving into my typical rash foolhardy actions. If I did train in this condition, it would be self-defeating on two fronts. Firstly it would compound health issues and make recovery period longer and secondly, damage traces of confidence that I'd built up to date. It was sensible to wait until good health returns and start up again. It felt quite strange fighting the urge to get up and go, but I resisted it.

A week later and still not 100% fit with a lingering headache, stuffed up nose but with the coughing and wheezing having subsided it was a ripe time for action. After further mild medication and a good breakfast, it was a man on the brink of a 'raring to go' state to take on the challenge of swimming again.

I arrived at the pool at 9:45 as always fifteen minutes before officially opening. There was only one other swimmer there before me. I had met this man on the previous visit to the pool. He knew I was English and insisted we speak English; God bless him. It was, therefore, an English conversation we had throughout the process of changing into our swimming gear. The insistent chatting continued into the showers and then into the pool. With this focus on communication, it was distracting trying to concentrate on the routine of getting ready to swim. It is strange speaking English nowadays as I rarely do and when it does happen, I have to think twice to avoid slipping back into Bulgarian words and phrases. There was no way I could multi-task with his request for me to correct his less than perfect English alongside trying to focus on relaxing and warming up before I entered the pool respectively. There was never an opportunity to keep my earplugs in. Every time they were put in, the talking started up again and reluctantly had to be taken out on each occasion. The unplugging happened on numerous occasions due to his enthusiasm and rare opportunity to speak and practice his English with a native Englishman was overwhelming. There was no way I could ignore his passion and spoil his moment being the gentleman I am.

He told me his name was Kolo as he finally glided away into another swimming lane to get his bi-weekly swimming fix. It was with some relief when he did leave me alone. No offence to Kolo, but I was frustrated at that point not being able to follow my planned training prelude routine.

Now with some time to think about what I needed to do, there was a tendency to rush everything to try and make up lost time. There was a little panic before I began to warm up with some bobbing exercises. Bobbing didn't come naturally today and it was some while before the sequence became familiar and felt at ease.

The next drill was just warming up with some manageable breaststroke lengths with my head underwater every two strokes. The breaststroke again felt uncomfortable and I struggled with the breathing sequencing. It was difficult to get relaxed and with this, I subsequently gave up on the head under every two strokes to get rid of stress. To my credit, I did manage six lengths without getting too exhausted. It was a surprise when I worked out that I had covered over 100 metres! It wasn't continuous having to stop and turn each length, regardless of this, I don't recall going this far in any of the previous sessions so I'll call that progress.

My goggles were always steaming up and the rubber straps slipping, making them loose and causing water to seep in. They were the cheapest goggles in the world so there shouldn't be complaints. With Kolo as a distraction, I had hadn't smeared the lenses with washing up liquid. This smearing system I bring along with me in my kit is in the form of a tissue infused with the washing up liquid and stored in a plastic bag to stop any evaporation. I decided to get out of the pool and go back into the changing rooms for the googles to be smeared with the thought of one less issue in contention.

Shortly afterwards, it was back in the pool for the next drill with the kickboard. As before it was working on the left arm front crawl and breathing to my left each stroke while rolling my body at the same time. It felt very uncomfortable today and caused panic initially. Eventually, I managed to complete a full length and although stressed at the end, better than previous attempts. With this landmark under my belt, I tried to do the same routine without the kickboard. I failed miserably only completing only four metres before panic set in and an immediate stop; A bad moment. Back to the kickboard again and continued working on this until I felt a bit more at ease.

At about this time, a middle-aged woman had got into the pool and began sharing my lane. No big deal for me, although I had to time my lengths just as she arrived at my end each time to avoid nervy passing by. It only took a little wait before pushing off each time. She asked me where I got my earplugs from as she didn't have any. I explained I bought them on eBay from China and had to wait six weeks for them to arrive. She told me that she was having problems with water running into her ears. I know how she feels with this issue having similar headaches without them to the point of not being able to go in the water without earplugs. I suggested she tried a spare pair I had in my kit. This particular pair of earplugs had come with the cheap goggles I bought. She was more than content as I gifted them to her. She immediately plugged them in, thanked me and swam off again. Well, I was just as pleased as her by having helped her, albeit she probably has the cheapest earplugs in the world.

The kickboard exercises continued; only this time, I tried out the right arm and breathing on the right side. I had failed miserably in the previous session, not being able to last more than two strokes before panic and feet grounded. With more composure and being more prepared mentally ready to relax brought about a result – a whole length completed! A significant achievement for me. The state of relaxation did fade quickly was non-existent by the end of the length. However, it was better than anything else before. Dwelling on my success, it was back to the left strokes and left breathing again with the kickboard and feeling less stressed out with this favoured side.

I felt a little more confident that progress now had been seen. The session finished slightly earlier as it felt like I was 'hanging on'. Mentally it felt like I could have metaphorically fallen off the edge of the cliff at any moment with panic over those last few minutes. Knowing I can't swim front crawl with the proper technique, style and breathing without a floating aid was still a daunting thought. However, I am determined to push myself with this; there are no alternatives to being able to swim front crawl. Beyond this, it will just be a matter of working on fitness. There is, as I have quickly discovered, a different kind of conditioning needed in swimming.

During the session, my goggles straps continued to work themselves loose filling with water. This negativity turned out to be quite convenient, giving a reason to stop and break in the swimming drills. This inconvenience also gave thinking time and moments to recompose. The distraction of adjusting the straps each time was, therefore, a healthy psychological aid. Conveniently, I used this as an alibi while other swimmers look on seeing me tightening of the strap as the reason for the pause. Being highly strung is one of my attributes.

When I got home, I found that my goggles had a plastic fastening component missing. This part was needed to hold and lock the strap in place. It must have happened in the shower after had finished the session. I recall dropping them on the floor before packing them away. I now have a pair of goggles that need a double knot to keep one side of the rubber strap on and I can see the same thing happening to the other side. I will have to get another pair although it might take a few days to arrive by post as there are no sources of decent goggles in our town after a big shopping hunt previously.

On reflection, despite still not feeling recovered from flu, today was a session where I saw an improvement. It was just a trickle, but progress nevertheless. There is a long way to go, but you can't eat an elephant all in one go.

Best Session to Date

After a terrible night with lingering flu continuing and persistently annoying cough, it wasn't a good sign for the day ahead. By the time the alarm went off at 07:00, it felt like I hadn't got any sleep at all. It was a quick breakfast and back to bed for an hour rather than practice the piano, which is the routine. By Jove, I needed that extra hour!

Over the last 48 hours, there was a lot of looking up online tutorials on breathing technique drills. There are many views from experts out there trying their darned best to inspire beginners. They make it look so easy, there must be at least one method that might work with me, but there were now many drills for breathing implanted into my head to the point of confusion. Today's session, the intention was to focus on just one or two of them to start.

The mind boggles on how many goggles are out there for sale online. Looking up the hundreds of reviews to find the best-suited goggles is a massive headache down to the sheer quantity of varieties out there. Goggles that will give more confidence and one less worry was the objective but on a low budget. I know reviews are geared towards marketing and selling with some reviews often are bought by sellers, so I have a sceptical view of most, if not all reviews published.

There are outlets here in Bulgaria that have stocks of many swimming goggles, but at hugely inflated prices. I understand that buying a pair of goggles for £10 in the UK and with the cost of postage that doubles that price to £20. The same set of goggles online here in Bulgaria retail at the same rate as the UK was inclusive of postage, i.e. £20. However, this does annoy me, as the postage cost for bulk goods is substantially cheaper than individual items. Yet, buying online in Bulgaria has advantages. Firstly, the goods arrive within two days and there is less risk of them getting lost or damaged. Secondly, if they are faulty, it wouldn't cost an arm and a leg to return them to the supplier for a refund or another pair. With these advantages in mind, a pair of goggles were ordered online with a Bulgarian online shop. Wise as we are to deals and promotions, my partner Galia added some cosmetics to the order. The reason being that goods purchased over the 50 leva qualifying for free postage. The goggles ordered were a pair of Arena Zoom X-Fit in green and black and the cost 32 leva.

Goggles Galore, but Expensive

They arrived on Thursday in time for my Friday training session. It was an exciting moment trying them out, especially so having suffered lots of grief from the original pair I bought. Alongside running repairs and adjustments, it was like a torture chamber wearing the old goggles and a massive relief taking them off. The new pair should now give me a chance to focus entirely on swimming. Although until I have tested in the pool, I won't know. The old goggles were packed in my swimming kit to use for the last time with a 'swan song' before the new pair arrives. Then they will be packed as a reserve pair.

There was only one other elderly swimmer in the pool when I arrived at the pool. The swimmer was not the enthusiastic English speaking Kolo who I usually encounter on Monday and Friday sessions so no distractions today.

The attention today was all about being calm and relaxed and not rushing anything. Rushing has been a lifetime's habit I still pursue. This hurriedness was a common trait each time I prepare the swimming kit before leaving home, also the walk to the pool and got changed ready to swim. A quick rethink about not rushing and everything slowed down to plan at this point. I felt calm now as I showered before dipping into the warm pool. There is always that little apprehension knowing there will be times ahead in the session when the calms disappear and panic situations take over. It is just a case of trying to make sure they become less frequent.

Bobbing is always first in line as a drill. As the ups and downs, inhaling and exhaling repeated, they got faster as I felt more comfortable. Speeding this drill up was suggested by swimming Gurus and taken up on this occasion. It hadn't got to the stage of not having to think about it. There is a build-up of a rhythmic sequence needed before going onto the next step. The big point here is it helps to put you in a relaxed state before the next stage of warming up.

A few lengths of breaststroke is also now part of the routine warming up. The objective here was also to do the breaststroke with head underwater every two strokes. There was a certain uncanniness that the rhythm of breathing here just the same as in the bobbing drill earlier. I tried not to rush the strokes and relax. There were eight lengths achieved with a slight pause to turn each time. After swimming 136 metres, I was not exhausted, although just a little out of breath and a slight rise in heart rate. There were only two sets of panic both towards the end of a length. When rushing with the end of the length in sight, the calm, slow and rhythmic sequence of breathing is lost, tension rises, leading to a panic moment.

Two waves of panic aside, I was warmed up and a little chuffed with the distance covered. It was over a third more than the 100 metres I did in the last session. The thought of now moving onto the front crawl made me feel nervous. Front crawl breathing drills were going to give the highest risk of intake of water, subsequent panic and abrupt stops. The last session saw progress, so why should there be more today?

Before I started, there were some more bobbing drills to bring back the relaxed state again, ready to begin front crawl technique drills. This drill was holding on to the side of the pool wall with both hands. Then putting my head face down under the water and breathing out of my nose. While this is happening, I make a stroke with the left arm. My head then turns left, coming up for breath after each cycle. The aim was to get my head is only half out of the water for each breath. Each time my head turned, I made a point of making less of a turn of the head. I didn't manage to turn my head only half out of the water, which was the objective, but it was getting quite close towards the end.

There was another tip I picked up online was to force air out of your nose and mouth before the head turns out of the water. This system clears the mouth and nose from the water before the intake of breath. It seemed to make sense to me as the panics happen when there is already water in my nose, then my head turns for breath. That standing water can only go further up my nose and inhaled. Low behold, I tried this for a few minutes and it worked! Breathing in with no water lurking in the mouth or the nostrils was salvation. The thought now was to take this technique onto the next stage with the floating aid.

Left-arm strokes only with a slight body, turn to give room for the head to rotate and breathe on the left. This was just like the previous drill on the side of the pool. This time though it was with the kickboard held in front and moving forward. It was an ecstatic Martin who now felt quite confident doing this drill. There were a few moments when I felt panic coming on, but these happened exclusively coming towards the end of each length. Seeing the finish line approaching, prompts a rush and the rhythm disappears. These were the same symptoms as in the breaststroke earlier.

I still feel I need more time on this particular drill. The time required is just to get it automated, not having to force my concentration. Also, work on finishing lengths at the same tempo as the start retaining that calm and steady rhythm. It is encouraging now as I complete most lengths not getting exhausted but just a little short of breath probably from the tendency to spurt towards the end of each length.

There was an attempt now doing the same drill but without a kickboard. I attempted this with the right arm extended out as if the kickboard wasn't there. I didn't feel comfortable with this at all as my head was lower in the water. In consequence, I had to use more energy to get my head up to make room above water for breathing. It just felt very uncomfortable and nervy, leaving me feeling vulnerable. I gave up after one length as I knew I wasn't ready for this stage yet.

The session was finished off with a couple of lengths of easy breaststroke, then out of the pool after 45 minutes. I knew that this session was the best to date even though I left on a low note by giving up on the last drill. There is a much more confident person now knowing that each time I make progress no matter how sluggish.

It may take one or two months to get into a conventional front crawl stroke without having to overthink about the breathing technique. Then the fitness and stamina can be tackled – That right now is a long way away. The doubts of not being able to complete the 2-mile swim in September have somewhat diminished now. There were 136 metres achieved today non-stop, only 3,064 extra metres to go. Also, there was the arrival of the new goggles on Friday to entertain me.

New Goggles Arrived

My new goggles arrived today and it was an excited man collecting them from the local private delivery office. The water-glasses came alongside a couple of other cosmetic goods for Galia to qualify for free postage. I opened the packer carefully and read the instructions two or three times over, a deliberate precaution not to rush and rip up the packaging. Many a time stuff has been ruined by tearing the packaging and not reading instructions correctly. In this case, I was fully aware of my ignorance in this new sport of swimming and the new alien equipment arriving needed to be reviewed and fully understood.

Wearing these new goggles for the first time felt very uncomfortable and this was a worry thinking that I had wasted my investment. The bridge of the goggles was rubbing on my nose. After adjustment as per the instructions, it felt more comfortable, but there was still a little constant rubbing sustained in this area. I just hoped it wouldn't irritate me too much wearing them over lengthy spells. There was no way I could test for leaking and fogging until I was actually in the pool, but wasn't a long to wait for that to happen.

There was a birthday party the night before this training session and quite a few glasses of rakia, (Bulgarian homemade brandy) and beers were drunk. The drink accompanied with great homemade Bulgarian food that could have fed an army.

After a night of good company and the aforesaid festive treats, it was to bed with a broad smile on my face. I might add that we don't get usually get drunk on these occasions, we just get exhausted from the duration of the festivities. Commonly, parties here can last well over 24 hours. This one, however, didn't as we left early on this occasion. It is rare for us to leave parties early, we usually are the last to go, but there were two reasons for this. Firstly, in the back of my mind, there was the swimming session today and secondly, I wanted to watch live football that evening, namely Arsenal.

We got back in time for the second half as I watched my team win and to go through to the next round in the Europa Cup. Yes, I'm an Arsenal fan or more commonly a 'Gooner' and proud of that! Bed beckoned well after midnight but more than content with the conundrum of the events of the evening.

It was awake well before the alarm went off this morning due to one of our neighbours vacuuming their apartment at 06:20. We weren't feeling too good and very weary this morning, making the process of waking up being done in slow motion. Dodgy stomachs also hit us both for some unknown reason. The tiredness still rolled on even after getting away from the dreamy world of bed! Drinking hot ginger, lemon and honey-infused tea consumed didn't make much difference to how we felt. There had to be something to eat if I was to go training in the pool today. Cold leftover pasta filled me up and it was back to bed for an hour or so before making my way to the high school. During this return to bed, there was no sleep with the countdown to the training session ticking away loudly in my mind. I was repeatedly going over the swimming and breathing drills I had planned in the pool later.

With some discomfort with my stomach and leaving Galia in our sickbed, it was not long before I arrived at the pool. There is a little routine now each time I make my way there. Next to the school, where the pool is the situated is a public car parking lot alongside a taxi rank. I have to walk through the car park to access the entrance to the school. There is a ticket machine there where you have to pay for parking. The ticket machine has a digital clock and each time I pass this, I look to see what the time it is. The school pool opens officially at 10:00 but allows swimmers in at 09:45. Being English means that time plays an integral part in most, if not all daily routines. Essentials with time are contrary to Bulgarian culture. They feel comfortable and relaxed being too early or more often late; unlike me. The time shown on this ticket machine is a remedy for this somewhat irritable English syndrome of an inbuilt need to be regimental with time. The earliest I arrived to-date was 09:37 where I sat down on a seat nearby to wait for the clock to show 09:44 before walking into the school grounds. From the ticket machine, it took just one minute to reach the receptionist in attendance and now on duty, therefore, an exact 09:45 arrival. The latest I had arrived was 09:50, which prompted a quick march with 'late' torturing my brain on that day. My aim is always to turn up at the parking ticket machine at the optimum time of 09:44.

There is a mobile phone I carry with me and conceivably I could use that as a tool for time, but it means opening my kit bag, fumbling about inside to find the phone and then put it all back when done. Too much fuss!

I was now in the changing rooms with another swimmer who arrived at the same time as me. We exchanged greetings, but it felt strange. I expected another person to be here, namely Kolo the incessant English speaking swimmer who attends on Mondays and Fridays. I wasn't sure whether this man here was Kolo and guessed it probably wasn't him as he wasn't speaking with me in English. Why wasn't I sure if I knew what he looked like? A simple explanation. There are roughly three or four men that attend the pool on a sporadic basis. All of these men are short, stocky about the same age (middle-aged) with the same short and thinning grey hair. I am short-sighted and without my glasses, everything more than a few feet away looks blurred. These men in question if seen more than a couple of metres away from me all look the same. It remained a mystery as to who this other swimmer was, but other clues as in him not talking to me led me to believe it wasn't Kolo.

Into the shower and pool finally to test out the new goggles with much trepidation. The dry testing yesterday at home wasn't too hopeful although much more comfortable than the previous pair. But then I don't think anything could have been worse than a couple of original instruments of torture! The bridge issue didn't seem to be a problem on this new pair; which was a relief. There was no fogging and being new of course meant that there was a crystal clear vision albeit will never correct to my short-sightedness. There were only a couple of times water penetrated through the seals, but it is just a matter of adjusting the tightness of the strap which I should master over time.

Into the first drill of bobbing and for some reason it didn't feel quite natural doing this today. I preserved for an extra few minutes to try and get that feeling of not having to think about it. It gradually came about and gave license to move onto the warm-up session of breaststroke.

Ten lengths of breaststroke swam today in the warm-up. One hundred seventy metres non–stop with head under every two strokes was achieved and only one moment of panic towards the end. Reduced panic moments is encouraging, with just a little fatigue felt and nowhere near exhausted. It seems a prolonged warm-up drill is beneficial. The only down part of this was the incredibly slow pace made. I just don't understand why moving forward is sluggish, as I watch other swimmers in the pool doing the same stroke and seemingly the same technique as me and they travel past me at twice the speed. Notwithstanding, I put this to the back of my mind for now and move on to the next drill.

Bobbing was brought back again, which this time felt more natural and more comfortable than before. The next drill was to have both arms holding onto the side of the pool, breathing in and exhaling with the left arm doing front crawl strokes with my feet firmly on the floor. It felt effortless, in fact too easy so I didn't dwell too long on this. There was a time however when I recall that this drill was not as easy as it was today, so there was a feel-good factor that kicked in.

I picked up a kickboard and used it with left arm strokes and left side breathing with a passive right arm. This drill felt good as I completed a few lengths. Water up the nose happened but was now becoming a rarer event. After each length finished, I paused to recover for about 10-15 seconds before starting up again. There was some labouring with my breathing and the breaks needed. Guess this is due to lack of swimming fitness, not general fitness which I'm sure this will improve over time.

There was an attempt to work on the right-side breathing with a dormant left arm. It didn't feel natural and brought about some panic when tried. I know with practice, this will become more comfortable and natural, so, not too stressed about this right now.

Many swimming experts online say you don't move on to the next drill until you are comfortable with the previous one. With Guru advice taken, it was back to more left arm strokes and left side breathing continuing with the kickboard. It was good to feel comfortable with this drill now. By putting in an additional stroke with the right arm while still only left breathing, I made a transgression. Each hand that isn't on a stroke is on the kickboard. This drill wasn't consistent and needed more practice, but at least I know which exercise has to be worked on and a stage further on to where I was on the last session.

Being the devil I am, I thought I'd try the drill with just the left arm and left side breathing without a kickboard float. On reflection, this was a bad idea and I wished I hadn't gone into it. Severe panic and anxiety took hold after just a few strokes and it was apparent I wasn't ready for this just yet!

Finally, there were two lengths of breaststroke to finish off, leaving me a little tired. To check the time, I had to get out of the pool to be nearer to the clock to see more clearly with my short-sightedness.

When the hand of the clock came into focus, I worked out that it had been a 50-minute session, much longer than previous sessions.

Showered, dried, dressed and walking home the feeling was good. Another little step forward to solving the front crawl breathing technique. As long as this continues like it has been and not worrying about how long it takes the fears of swimming and water can take a little step backwards. The 2-mile swim in September was always on my mind. If I have to use breaststroke or a snorkel, so be it. Whatever it takes to get that swimming medal and London Classics medal respectfully.

Spa Centre Holiday with a Pool

The plan each week was to have three sessions of swimming, namely Monday, Wednesday and Friday. The advice given online was to make sure that there is time for recovery of 48 hours between sessions which fits in nicely with this plan. At weekends the school swimming pool is closed, but that doesn't affect anything. Besides, it wouldn't be fair on Galia with the limited free time she has at the weekend for us to do things together.

This 48-hour recovery got me thinking. Reading up on the techniques of swimming, I invariably come across triathlon features. I'd never seriously thought about a triathlon challenge before now, as swimming was a big put off and a fearsome goal. Give me a pair of running shoes or a bike and I'd be a happy soul running or riding. Give me a pair of swimming trunks and my heart would sink with fear. Until now, swimming has been a taboo activity and avoided wherever possible. Maybe once this current challenge of learning how to swim is under my belt, a triathlon just might be something to contemplate. The point of this 48-hour recovery needs a revisit here. How can three events be trained for with a 2-day recovery period? Something worth trying to figure out if a triathlon is on the cards next year.

Last Friday's planned training session didn't happen due to a sleepless night due to a searing pain in my right shoulder. Lack of sleep was something that I didn't need having made some progress in recent swimming sessions. It was a mystery as to how and where shoulder pain came about. I do weight training three times a week and a minimum of 5-minute plank routines daily with thorough warming-ups and warm downs made. It, therefore, couldn't be from these exercises as I've never been injured or sore from these routines. Galia thinks it could be a cold draft I commonly subject myself to in bed. At night I sleep without a blanket or duvet over me due to being too hot. Then fall asleep only to wake up a few hours later, freezing! All said and done, I took some paracetamol in the morning and the pain eased up slightly by lunchtime. By mid-afternoon, I was pruning trees on the farm with hardly any pain.

With the severe shoulder pain overnight and in the morning, we decided that we should go on a three-day break to a Spa Centre to relax, chill out and get a little detoxification. There was a little concern about the lack of swimming this week given having already missed a session. We searched for a Spa Centre that had a decent-sized indoor pool and it wasn't long before we found one. It was in one of our favourite places in Bulgaria called Hisarya. We had been there three times before, but only to small mineral indoor pools to bathe not designed for swimming. The hotel we opted for had a 12-metre mineral pool which was big enough to at least to get in a few lengths of swimming drills.

We arrived Sunday afternoon. Before we even unpacked our cases, it was into the sauna, jacuzzi and the warm thermal water-filled pool which registered at 28C. With no swimming aids such as kickboards, it was bobbing, breaststroke and front crawl with just left side breathing as practised in the Yambol pool back home. There was quite a bit of dodging children, but it felt comfortable albeit much shorter lengths with short recovery pauses at each end. This need for a time for recovery after each length is beginning to worry me. For sure, this was a sign that the front crawl technique is not working effectively. It is only breathing on the left side that doesn't feel too uncomfortable. When trying breathing the right side, my mouth and nose fill up with water and the inevitable feet to the ground with panic takes place. Being a very dominated left-footed and left-handed, it is not a big surprise that it feels clumsy and awkward trying thing out on the right side. The plan was to address this once back on my home training ground in Yambol.

We were here to relax and chill out, so I didn't focus too much on training drills. It was, therefore, a resigned mood trying to enjoy the swims and get in with some easily sustainable breaststroke. Galia was quite surprised at my swimming feats having last seen me trying to swim like a landlubber in the Black Sea last year. It inspired her to try a bit of front crawl herself. It is quite strange that I could see what she should be doing to improve her front crawl technique. It was as if I was now a swimming Guru after extensive research and first-hand attempts with the disciplines. Her style was the same as mine was a few weeks ago. Her head always up out of the water, lots of splashing strokes with flailing arms and ending up exhausted after a few metres. I could relate to that to a tee. However, she decided to return to breaststroke after I offered her some advice with front crawl style. I didn't want to force anything on her if she was happy returning to and sticking by breaststroke. Again, I can see the appeal of this relaxed and non-panicky stroke.

The Swimming Pool in Hisarya

Each day over the three days countless lengths were completed. Also added to this was a little experiment trying to kick turn at each end of the length. Each attempt failed miserably each time with complete disorientation every single time with underwater half summersault and trying to kick me off against the wall. Not too worried about this though, but will try to get this mastered once the front crawl breathing and sound technique is in order.

These new goggles were giving me a little grief. They began to let in water and fog up consistently. The extent of this was starting to annoy me and affect my mood in the water. Each length that went by, the goggles I had to empty the water and I couldn't wipe away the fogging as the instructions advised not to touch the inside of the lenses. This inconvenience continued for the first two days. On the third day, I decided to do the toothpaste trick for the fogging. Also, some major tampering took place with the tightness of the strap. Hey presto, no fogging and after a few more adjustments on the straps, both issues disappeared. Why I didn't do this on the first and second days remains a mystery and was annoyed with myself for not doing this earlier.

The 3-day break was a good idea, although we probably put some weight on during that time. Despite swimming, there were big continental breakfasts first thing in the morning followed by a couple of lunchtime beers. The refreshments were welcome blessed with hot weather on this break. Then, more drinking and eating throughout the long evenings, which is what happens when you choose all-inclusive on holiday deals.

Back home in Yambol on Wednesday refreshed and ready to get back into the training regime. The plan was to visit the pool the very next day to try and make more progress.

Back in the Local Pool

The 07:00 alarm didn't get a chance to sound as I woke up at 06:35 with high intent to getting back into the local pool today has been on my mind throughout the night.

The parking ticket machine showed 09:45 today on arrival, so without any pause, it was a quick march into the school swimming block and paid the 3 leva fee to the regular woman cashier. I am sure she had thought I had given up swimming, having not seen me for six days. There was a lonely but entirely focused Martin changing into his swimming gear being the only one in the changing room. Through to the shower room with a cold rinse and into the pool where the still, empty waters greeted me.

Somehow it felt quite nervy getting into the water caused by the thoughts of the drills I was about to practice today knowing I would be out of my comfort zone. As always, bobbing is the beginning of the warm-up. It didn't feel natural even though I ran it into extra time to try and cure this. I still wasn't relaxed when I went into the warm-up session of breaststroke lengths. With the head under every two strokes, there was no sense of calmness or relaxing and it wasn't long before the first gulp of water experienced. The gulp led to a panic stop that took place on the second length! In recent times this wasn't normal as I tried to figure out why this was, but couldn't at this point.

Perseverance prevailed with more forced lengths mustered. The record to date was 12 lengths non-stop, but on this occasion, I lost count. Even so, I was sure it was more than 12, possibly 14 or 16.

The problem of losing count of lengths was something I wondered about before. Counting up to 15 or 20 lengths is feasible, but when it gets beyond these numbers is difficult and getting into three-figure numbers would be near on impossible. How can you keep track? There are hi-tech watches that count swimming lengths and running laps, but I'm not keen on watches, besides it would feel like another stranglehold and an additional claustrophobic element on my wrist. The initial idea on how to solve this logistic problem was to firstly, time how long it took to swim a length. Then, swim and time how long the whole swim took. Finally, divide the time it took for one length into the time for the overall swim. The calculation should give the number of lengths completed. With a clock high up on the wall in the pool area, there was no need for a watch. However, this system is not needed just yet with the number of lengths only in their teens. The only disadvantage is not being able to see the clock from the pool with my poor eyesight.

The drill plan today was using kickboard leading the way with left side arm strokes and left side breathing. To my amazement, this went well feeling reasonably comfortable and relaxed. It felt more natural this time and not forced, which was pleasing as that was the main objective. It just needs to be more consistent in terms of refining the breathing into a non-rushed manner rather than trying to gasp air before my head goes under again frantically. Currently, it is a great sense of relief after each time an intake of breath is managed. There is a clear message of thought after each breath, essentially saying to myself 'wow, I got away with it this time!' Throughout this drill, there was that reoccurring thought nagging me. Still, within the bounds of time spent practising this it was a vast improvement from the first attempts at this drill a few weeks ago.

After reading up on advice with breathing, it now it quite apparent that breathing on one side alone with front crawl is not good for your health. It puts you at a disadvantage in open waters. The plan was to master breathing on one side then build this up on the opposite side to achieve a bilateral breathing system. This option of switching sides whenever the need arises is a big plus here. Once again, armed with a kickboard, it was now an attempt to use the same drill but on the right side as the comfort zone suddenly disappeared.

As predicted, it all went pear-shaped after only two strokes with water taken in, panic stations and an abrupt stop with feet firmly on the ground. I tried again and again, but it was torturous mentally. Eventually, I managing a length with significant discomfort, a flapping style and felt exhausted when finally reaching the pool wall. This drill needs to be worked upon in future sessions as I am determined to get it to feel just like the left side. The consequence of not having an option right now to use the right side breathing technique frightens me a little.

Back with the kickboard again and a few lengths using left and right alternative breathing. No surprise to find it okay on the left and panic experienced each time it was right side's turn. It felt like a cyclic homecoming and relief each time I returned to the breathing on the left side!

The session ended with a couple of warm down breaststrokes lengths. I felt this session was constructive, albeit with many ups and downs giving rise to varying degrees of confidence. There was a way to think about this, namely relating and reflect as to how it was not so long ago and how it is now. That is an excellent antidote to feeling down in confidence and rids any despondence.

Looking at other swimmers that had now joined me in the pool, it was quite easy to spot their mistakes. Their seemingly faultless gliding through the water manner when I first saw them has now become less than perfect in my eyes. They are still miles better than anything that I can muster up; it has to be said. Nevertheless, it is so easy to diagnose technical issues looking in, but arduous with the attempts of self-diagnosis. Maybe I'll get Galia to video me one day and I can tear myself apart with the same criticism. It won't happen until the front crawl breathing is sorted, which shouldn't take a lifetime!

I can swim

Having swum two days in a row without the recommended 48-hour recovery does not worry me in the least. The effort I put into the sessions isn't enough to make me feel exhausted or weary; it is just psychological exhaustion. Cycling and running take more out of me due to the extra effort put in, the length of time in action and without breaks or pauses for the most. Riding my bike for 5-6 hours or running for over an hour non-stop would undoubtedly benefit with a 48-hour recovery, although this was rare when I was training in those disciplines. Just a 50-minute swim, inclusive of warming up, warming down with lots of breaks each length and between drills doesn't warrant a two-day recovery period.

So just a 24-hour break it is then. It is off to the pool and standing at the parking ticket machine at 09:46 precisely. The arrival was a minute later than yesterday and I know why. Taking the rubbish out of our apartment and dump it in the wheelie bins provided in the street took that minute in time. There was a short diversion involved of 100 metres before joining the usual route to the pool. Funny how you can account for almost every second when having been brought up on culture with strict time-base. That is so English.

The changing room was empty when I entered. I had expected to see Kolo and his insistent request for me to speak English, but he wasn't there. To be quite honest, it was a bit of a relief as I could now focus entirely on preparing for the swim. If my swimming technique was sound and I was here just for a build-up of swimming distance and endurance getting the miles in, then I would welcome the talking, but not just yet.

It felt nervous each time I entered the water once again knowing that there are going to be moments of discomfort with water up the nose and take in the mouth on some of the drills planned. From my little experience in water, I was now fully aware that a proper warm-up routine is essential, achieving a relaxed state before attempting any of the drills later on reducing panic situations.

Bobbing today was much more comfortable than yesterday, but there is still that thought of what if I breathe in underwater? With this thought, there is almost a sense of daring myself to do it. I don't know why this occurs. It makes no sense at all thinking about doing or daring yourself to do something that will cause hurt or distress. The more I think about it, the bigger the dare becomes, which was probably the mainstay problem in my previous session. Today, fortunately, this mind wondering was just briefly fleeted in and out.

Breaststroke today was done on a timed manner rather than counting the lengths. I set a time of 10 minutes and started on this new timed format. Strange how when I was counting the lengths yesterday I lost count, but today I tried to lose count but couldn't! After 10 minutes, I had covered ten lengths. Not as many lengths as before, but today I wanted to focus more on front crawl drills and not too much time spent on breaststroke. Besides, it was enough to warm me up prepared for the next more demanding exercise.

The kickboard was now in my hand, but not until another session of bobbing took place to bring back into a more relaxed frame of mind. Soon it was into left side strokes and breathing for two lengths to get into the mode. It felt much more comfortable and more natural now with this left side drill. There seemed fewer instances of water intake the more it went on. It was time to work on the weak right side after these good moments. After all, this was my main focus today.

It felt awkward on the right side and had to stop a few times in panic due to tensing up and not breathing calmly. I was trying to bring my head up too far and was gasping for air. The problem was that this was done in a rushed manner, far removed from being relaxed and certainly not done in a controlled manner. Trying to write with the opposite hand gives out a clumsiness and awkwardness and that is exactly how it felt with this drill. To give me a little lifeline here, I decided to continue with the kickboard and do a session of using alternative left/right strokes. Also counting 'one thousand,' 'two thousand,' 'three thousand.' before each alternative stroke and breathing side. There was a great sense of relief finishing each length. However, it worked out better than I thought it would and glad my perseverance pay off.

Next, it was back onto the right side again where surprisingly after a few strokes, the breathing felt less panicky. Trying to replicate those first few moments was awkward, but I pushed myself to try and get this done on a more consistent basis. There was a little breakthrough here, but considering this is the first week of getting the right side up and running I didn't want to overkill the drill and stopped while in a positive mental mood.

As a reward, I decided to try and swim the front crawl without a kickboard, just breathing on the left. The first length was done with relative ease as I touched the wall at the end of the first length. A slight pause taken gave rise to a sudden realisation - I was now swimming front crawl with correct breathing technique for a whole length and there was no stress or panic involved at all. It is only the left side breathing, but a front crawl style that works. It has evolved and potentially I could use this in drills based on endurance, not technique. It felt like I had arrived at a point where I had achieved the first goal towards making the 2-mile swim in front crawl.

The next step was to swim without a kickboard and a dare to breathe every three strokes, essentially this was bilateral breathing. However, this was a step too far for me as I sunk, panicked and grounded my feet after only a few metres. The weak and lousy technique on the right side was the reason. It needs much more work on to get it somewhere near to natural as the left.

There is still some way to go with the bilateral breathing, but this was being worked on and would be the final step to just getting swimming fitness in order. I try not to think about the other issues swimming in open water with lots of other swimmers knocking, splashing and barging. There is still a long road ahead to get my swimming 'streetwise' and overcome the fear of water which has dogged me all my life.

I finished with two lengths of smooth but painfully slow breaststroke to warm down. The second length to my surprise saw me gulp in water and stop for some reason beyond me. With this hiccup, I left the pool, forcing myself to think of the progress had been made with the earlier drill before that final warm-down.

The next session is planned after the weekend on Monday, working on the right-side breathing again. It was unusual for me to look forward to it and strangely not as nervous and apprehensive as on previous occasions.

Swimming Fitness Edging In

The next session planned to take place on Monday didn't happen. Business got in the way with an appointment with a solicitor in the morning, which was unavoidable.

We are looking after Galia's Grandson all this week and as you would expect additional chores attached, so I set this morning's alarm for an earlier time of 06:00. We were both awake before that torturous din! Two sleepless nights in a row and exhausted with a two-year-old that we had to get to kindergarten by 07:30. Having completed babysitting chores, this left me free time up until 17:00. Then it will be another trip to the kindergarten, this time for a child collection.

It was now 09:45 as I paused by the parking ticket machine, then the short walk straight through the school playground where the pool is situated. A flight of six steps leads into the pool building block to pay the fee of 3 leva. Being English, it is always the word 'please' said in the asking and a 'thank you' on receiving the small receipt. These equivalent wordful manners are generally not used here in Bulgaria, thus giving away my English traits even when speaking Bulgarian.

Now into the changing room where any sound gave an echo; an excellent place for singing or playing my viola reminiscent old church hall acoustics. It is all calm but a little eerie to have the place to myself. There is no rush to get set up and no distraction from other swimmers, old or young. Bitterly cold water always greets me being the first in the shower room. It takes a good minute before any warm water comes through, but I don't dwell. It was knowing that open water events are exclusively in cold water, a move to get used to being immersed cold water is something that I now practise. Not pleasant, but part of the training. I don't think it gets easier with practice either having done this many times before here in the school shower; even on the first day. The initial 10 seconds are the worst as anyone who has gone through this knows. The freezing water just numbs your body, but after that, there is a bonus. When stepping into the pool, it now feels like a hot bath.

I always put my cap on before showering as the one time I didn't it was difficult and painful trying to get it off with wet hair. My googles aren't put on until I am in the pool and soaked. I remembered to smearing on and buff off toothpaste this morning, so one less worry with the expectation no fogging and there wasn't!

It was bobbing for a few minutes to get the breathing routine up and running although it took quite a few bobs to get into an autopilot state. Once that had been achieved, it was a 10-minute breaststroke session with the focus on getting my head under the water a little deeper than before to get into a more streamlined body position. This improved, sleek bodyline should help gliding through the water faster. The trouble with trying to achieve this is the deeper your head goes down the further it has to come up for air, thus taking up more energy with this style. Not entirely sure whether it is effective from that point so I will have to experiment more and probably arrive at some form of compromise. No matter as the 10-minute swim taken, but there was an issue with my goggles causing me to stop several times. This problem was having to empty water that had seeped in. Each time I stopped to do that, the goggles were adjusted by tightening the strap further. It continued to give me grief. Now with a death grip hold in place with repeated tightening, I couldn't understand how water could get in. It was very uncomfortable tightness and accompanied by a fear that the strap would break with the strain and force given. These goggles were welded to my face. For now, it was something I just had to grin and bear.

It was time for the kickboard and breathing both on the right as well as my favoured left. This drill lasted over 30 minutes, with varying alternative right and left sides. The left to relax and the right always a struggle while trying to get accustomed to a more comfortable action to that alien side. What I did notice was that each length completed I didn't need as long to recover, in fact, on a few occasions quite easily turned and gone straight into another length. However, this was only when the left side breathing was in action. The right side is taking much more energy leading to many panic-ridden moments. Practice, practice and yet more practise more with this was the name of the game today.

The session was finished off with a couple of breaststroke lengths to wind down.

I have to admit, right-side breathing is going to take quite a while to master. It did improve today, but nowhere near to using this technique without the aid of a kickboard. Perseverance is the only answer.

Eventually, I got out of the pool and into the shower room. The water ran hot now as it had been running through the pipes used by other swimmers. The shower and pool water is heated up by solar panels covering the roof of the building. With this knowledge, there isn't any guilt in running the hot water to my heart's content with renewable energy in place. It also saves me having to shower at home so that 3 leva fee for the swim with inclusive shower makes it a better deal.

There is nothing quite like walking out into the bright warm sunshine after a swimming session and a shower to finish off. Feeling fresh and looking forward to a nice cup of coffee from a vending machine on the way home. Co-indecently there is a reminder of London on this vending machine on my regular refreshments after swimming sessions.

The Coffee Machine and a Reminder of London

The icing on today's cake was the thought of not being exhausted after the end of most completed lengths in front crawl. Conceivably this could be drawn from two points. Firstly improved swimming fitness, but more than likely down to better swimming technique with a more relaxed style, albeit with a kickboard. Looking back, this is a complete contrast to what was happening in the first sessions. There is still a long way to go, however.

Next due session is tomorrow after another 06:00 alarm call and the kindergarten drop off again. We just hope we get a good night of sleep, which hasn't happened since we started babysitting on Friday!

Chapter 3 (April)

Bit of a Downer Today

Yet another night of sleeplessness. Initially waking up at 02:20, I remained awake waiting for the alarm to go off at 06:00. Not sure why this is exactly, but nothing to do with swimming sessions.

Baby-sitting duties call again and back for another kindergarten drop off with Galia's Grandson. Then back home heavy-eyed with a nagging pain in my right shoulder which had plagued me sporadically over this last week. Sometimes the pain just disappears and other times it tortures me, strangely most painful when I lie down or sit down crouched over. Added to all this was a stomach upset for reasons beyond me. We are cautious in food hygiene and always eat fresh food and know what it contains. There is no fast food in sight for us - hence the mystery.

With all these issues put together, I know there was a message telling me to skip the pool session today. And that's what I thought I'd do as I laid down on the return to bed that saw no sleep earlier.

Dozing on and off and well aware of the time passing by, I just couldn't live with the guilt of skipping swimming today. If I didn't go, I'd be worse than I feel right now and sulk for the rest of the day and beyond. It was also the day for weight training and the usual daily plank exercises. Knowing me, if I skip swimming, it will lead to skipping other planned fitness routines. It was 09:20 and the decision made to get up and go. A few moments later, it was up on my feet and mustering my swimming kit. Galia tells me I am mad to have such a compulsion to swim when I was overly tired and ill.

Off I jolly well go to the swimming pool arriving at the parking ticket machine at precisely 09:43. Two minutes too early due to a brisk walking pace for some reason faster than usual. A pause, then moments later watching the bus that travels past at this time each visit with the same driver. That bus was the signal for entering the school grounds and forcing through the business of swimming. By this time, I had perked up a bit with the walk, my stomach was bearable and the right shoulder was just eking out a little pain.

All changed, a cold shower took being the first swimmer again today and ready to enter the pool semi-relaxed. I knew that this would be more challenging than most sessions due to the mind-set knowing I wasn't a well person.

The bobbing starts, which is something I quite enjoy as there is no threat of panic or fear now with this routine. It has taken a month to get this feeling and I use it to turn to combat anxiety at any point during other more demanding drills.

Breaststroke to warm up again for 10 minutes, this time just working on the breathing and head position. The aim was to use the least amount of energy raising my head and to breathe each third stroke. I did experiment with one breath each stroke, but that takes up more effort and is counter-productive, giving that up almost immediately. Knowingly there was no doubt in my head that I would eventually find a niche with this stroke and use it as back-up to the front crawl.

The front crawl comes to play now. I never knew it would be so demanding to get this stroke style sorted out. I don't know how much longer it will take to perfect the breathing which has been the ruin of enjoyment of this sport. Yes, I have to say I don't enjoy swimming from the point of being uncomfortable for 80% of the time. Having said that it was 98% of discomfort when I started. When there is a moment of getting something right, it is cause for celebration. Those little moments of achievement keep me on track.

However, today is a day when I took a step backwards with the drills of front crawl. I can only get stress-free swimming with the aid of a kickboard leading me off. There were countless lengths done with left, right and shared breathing sides with some consistency with the kickboard. Without the kickboard, it was disastrous, causing me to tense up, panic, stop numerous times and gathering my breath exhausted each time I completed a length. I just couldn't understand and get frustrated as to why, without the kickboard, my nerves get so jangled up.

Other swimmers in the pool are now a real point of interest. While bobbing, sometimes there is a pause underwater to view their styles of strokes and kicking motions. It just confuses me whether I should try and follow suit with the styles seen underwater here or stick to online advice from Gurus. These swimmers in the pool look so relaxed even with a less than perfect technique. I guess a lot is down to what you feel comfortable with; everyone is different. After all, the main objective from my point of view is to complete a 2-mile stretch of water with no competitive racing inclinations considered.

Dispelling race thoughts for me is difficult having a competitive nature. It was evident today when I was finishing a length with another swimmer moving up alongside me at a faster pace. I just couldn't help myself and pushed myself to beat him to the end. All the focus of the drill for technique and relaxation got thrown out of the window. Wanting to win was just against one swimmer in the pool, what happens if there are hundreds of potential competitors in the Serpentine Lake?

The session ended up with a step back in confidence. Knowing that after a month of training, I was still not able to do a front crawl swim without a floating aid was depressing. We all know that we have good and bad days and today was not a good day. More insult added to my emotion with the build-up of more pain in my right shoulder. There is hope that the next session may be better with a 48-hour recovery period leading up to it. There was time to get some much-needed sleep as well.

After the session finished, I was pleased that it had come to an end. I was still a joyful soul walking home and very thankful for the warm Bulgarian sunshine that followed and encompassed me. This joy stemmed from knowing that I had trained today despite all the signals telling me to forget the session. So, regardless of all the issues trying to put me off today, I was glad I went through the process as mentally, I felt better for it even though the session wasn't that good. Later on, the weight training and plank sessions also went ahead despite stomach cramps and right shoulder aching problems that had persisted throughout the day. Guess this is not surprising from someone who isn't a spring chicken anymore.

A classic quote by Doctor Zachary Smith from 'Lost in Space' comes to mind today. 'Oh the pain, the pain.'

'Yes' But Not 'YES!'

After half a bottle of red wine before retiring to bed, this seemingly gave way to a good night of sleep. Today, no babysitting, no aches or pains in the shoulder and glad to be alive for the continuation of the swimming challenge.

The 07:00 alarm woke me up after naturally waking up at 06:30 and dozing off again. Two boiled eggs, buttered toast soldiers and freshly brewed herb tea set me off for the start of a new day. Then, call me lazy, but it was back to bed again for breakfast to digest.

At 09:34, it was out of the front door and a well-timed walk and checking the parking ticket machine on arrival. It showed 09:45. The scheduled coach for this time rumbled past me as I entered the school premises.

All was going to plan as I entered the changing room, but there was something different here as I surveyed the room. Hanging up on the pegs on the wall were four sets of clothing and trainers tucked under the long benches that trailed along the wall. My mind immediately turned to logistics. There are four swimming lanes that they would all be in use, therefore sharing a lane could well be on the cards today. It was an issue for me, but maybe a more significant problem for more competent swimmers if I get in the way.

A little luxury of a warm shower was taken on the way to the pool with other swimmers using it earlier. Even though I opened up the cold tap on full, I could only get it to run lukewarm. This luxury did have a negative issue as now I would have to face the seemingly cold waters in the pool. I could easily get used to warm water showers, but that's not 'macho' and feels like a 'cop-out' on my eyes.

As I walked away dripping from the shower, I glimpsed into the pool area. There was water disturbance causing reflective discothèque light effects on the walls and ceiling. This magnificent effect was created by the strong morning sunlight shining and bouncing off the disturbed pool waters through the high windows. There was no time to boogie as I saw my regular nearside lane occupied by a swimmer. The side lanes are the last choice for good swimmers as both sides have two water filters that stick out along the length of the pool. This constriction creates less space to swim as you pass them. Also, there is a jet of fast water spurting out as you pass by, which pushes you away from the side. Quite often, especially with breaststroke, my hand would accidentally hit the filter system as I pass. On a few occasions, I have cut my hand on the metal corners. These obstructions in these lanes, therefore, are not favoured by most swimmers here. I, however, choose this lane as I feel safer near the side of the pool and essentially am considerate enough to leave the centre lanes for more competent swimmers – another English trait!

With my favoured side lane occupied, the far side lane wasn't. Fortunately, two of the swimmers were sharing an inside lane. I made my way to the far end lane and this remained solely in my possession throughout the swim.

Making sure my goggles were as 'tight as a duck's,' it was relaxing bobbing exercises for a few minutes. Then straight into the breaststroke, pleasant and comfortable with a focus on the smooth strokes and trying to stay relaxed. Ten minutes later, I was nicely warmed up and thinking I could do that all over again without getting weary. That thought was reassuring knowing that if all else fails two miles of pure breaststroke is a realistic option.

Bobbing a few more times again and enjoying it in preparation to go straight into the front crawl. The focus today was to practice more right-side breathing. Kickboard support was taken up initially with the left side stroke and breathing just to get up and running. It felt comfortable and familiar now - even natural! Then it was over to the right side. Yet again this felt so uncomfortable and awkward; at no point did I get a feeling of being relaxed.

Exhaustion and breathlessness occur after each attempted length purely down to bad technique and tension. There is no comparison the left-sided front crawl drills and I didn't enjoy this one bit.

Now and again I'd do a left side breathing to get the relaxing state back. The right side felt like being such a chore, but I know I have to push on until it gets comfortable and that's what keeps me going.

There is another factor involved here. My right shoulder is not as flexible as the left and has given me quite a bit of grieve in pain over the last few years. Even on my bike, I have to work on not putting pressure on the right side, which aches and creates numbness in my fingers. I am sure is why it feels tense on that side to the point of being somewhat disabled. It will never be the same as the left and I'd come to terms with that many years ago. But there has to be an effort made to try and improve that right side technique. Right now, there is no chance of me giving up on this.

Being comfortable on the left, it was now a drill without the kickboard with a few lengths breathing every two strokes. After a couple of lengths without any issues, it was a very pleasing thought to think I've almost got this 'cracked'. I even went to breathing every four strokes for a while just to check it out and it was possible.

Next step was to try the three strokes alternative breathing without the kickboard. There is a mindset issue here, as I know before I even start that this is going to be uncomfortable. For sure there will be some intake of water on the right side, tensing up, panicking and a stopping. I didn't want to go through this with that thought, but the dare was now on. True to expectations it was a struggle each time that right side breathing came in and such a relief to get back on the left again to recover. Stopping and feet to the ground often featured throughout.

After quite a few tense issues with this drill, I didn't want to end the session on this negative note. It was back to left side breathing again to finish off with only one nervy moment of water up the nose. I think this was due to getting tired at this point.

It was warming down with breaststroke again and the thought of how the session went compared to two days ago. If the previous session were 'chalk', then today would be 'cheese'! Two completely different outcomes from the sessions. It was a sense of a 'yes' I've cracked the front crawl, but not an elated 'YES!' due to the right side breathing requiring more work to master. Maybe some therapy outside the water is necessary with this.

With a free weekend ahead I was feeling good, despite today's little negative episodes!

Is Age Catching Up With Me?

All was going well after the last session some ten days ago, then something went 'click' and that was me out of action for a week. Sometimes there is a tweak felt in your back and within a split second, you know that continuous pain will follow for many days beyond. Simple actions like sitting down, sleeping at night, using the toilet, dressing and undressing then become significant tasks. During this period, there never seems to be any moment where the pain isn't present.

Grudgingly resigned to this situation; it was just a case biding my time going through the painful transition of the recovery period, which meant no swimming, jogging, cycling or gym work. It is difficult mentally not being able to do these things, even though I knew it was a short term hiccup in training. Throughout this period, the thought of maybe just doing a little workout kept digging into my brain. The resisting temptation of any form of physical activity was a struggle but eventually, it aided a swift recovery.

Not being a fan of taking drugs or medication, I finally gave in after my Galia insisted that I should consider taking painkillers for her sake. With my sleeplessness at night keeping her awake, it would be selfish not to. What helped most was a blend of Bulgaria Brandy (70% proof), hot chilli peppers and ground black pepper mixed and rubbed on the painful area on the base of my spine. Although I smelt like a distillery, it was far more effective than all these fancy and over-priced commercial painkilling drugs and rubs.

Each day that passed, there was a slight improvement. It was now a nervous man thinking that the next swimming session would be more difficult not having been in the water for ten days. My fears were ill-founded as I found out.

The car park ticket machine showed 09:44 and I arrived at the school dead on 09:45. It was Kolo, the incessant English speaker in the changing room. He was asking me whether I had any contemporary English poetry books for him to borrow. I said I didn't and even though in truth I had some in my comprehensive library of books at home. From my experience lending out books to people has on most occasions been the last time I'd ever see them. With this happened so many times, I have learned to think carefully and reflect on the possible consequences before committing to lending out any of my library books. Not that I didn't trust Kolo, it was just that I didn't want to tell myself 'I wish I hadn't' if my book collection further diminishes. My mind, however, was more on the pool and wondering how I'd feel after the long break.

I was first in the shower, a cold shower and then into the pool. My plan was just to focus what I felt comfortable with today and that was initially bobbing, breaststroke and front crawl working on the left side only. I practised all the drills in that order and the comfort zone came back straight away, which surprised me somewhat. There were just a few moments of water intake up the nose, which now didn't stop me as I continued without any panic or feet setting down. I know there will always be occasions of this happening, it is just a case of teaching myself not to panic and stop, but deal with it while maintaining the swim. During the whole session, there was only one moment my feet touched the pool floor, (other than turning around each end). There was a lingering thought knowing that there are only 17 metres to safety in the pool compared to the 2-mile stretch to safety in the event. This provocation of thinking is a psychological barrier to try and overcome or try to ignore as time goes on.

Some of my fears allayed itself after today's session. A renewed confidence that I can now begin to focus on swimming endurance rather than solely technical matters for the time being. Learning right-sided breathing in front crawl can wait a while as it consistently holds me back and digs a massive hole in confidence.

Mixing it

What is the time, Sir? 09:43 precisely and it was me at the car park ticket machine again, two minutes before opening time at the pool. What the hell I thought, I'll go in one minute early today and see what happens. On arrival, the receptionist refused to take my 3 leva fee saying that the pool wasn't open yet and I would have to wait. Being one minute early wasn't the problem; there was another issue. They were sorting out a matter of the pool's safety before opening today. Who am I to argue with that while waiting?

As I sat down on the bench by the side of in reception kiosk was after a short time joined in the wait by two other non-student swimmers. What inevitably goes through my mind again is whether there are eventually going to be more swimmers than lanes. Sharing a lane would be another step up to the open water swim with people as hazards and no rope barriers. This thought didn't make it feel too bad, as sharing space with other swimmers would be beneficial and appropriate if made out in training sessions.

We finally got the go-ahead to enter the pool after some 15 minutes. In the time that elapsed, four other swimmers had now gathered ready to take to the water. The nearside lane not favoured by other swimmers as mentioned before due to the two pumping filters that stick out that narrow the lane. Also, the torrent of water rushing out from the pump filters force you away from the wall side into the rope lane dividers. This flow simulates currents in many open waters, especially the sea and rivers; however, I doubt whether this would be an issue in still waters of the Serpentine Lake.

Today I did a few warm-up stretching exercises against the cold ceramic wall before entering the water. It was because I saw someone else doing it on the far side of the pool and it made complete sense on reflection. These stretching routines were very similar to what I use to do before getting into action cycling or running. I don't know why I didn't think of this before as I'd never ride or run without a warm-up routine.

After the stretching routine, there was a significant difference noticed once I entered into the water. With the additional out of water warm-up, there were only a few bobbing drills needed as I was more than ready to swim off with a 10-minute breaststroke warm-up.

The breaststroke is still slower than snail's pace despite experimenting with all variants of technique from the depth of the head in the water to the length of stroke and using different hand positions. There was also trying out new styles with the kicking. I altered the frog-leg style to becoming a more vertical and straight leg push. Nothing seemed to make any difference to speed apart from seemingly getting less drag when relaxed.

Front crawl is now more than manageable with the breathing style on the left side. Doing two lengths nonstop is possible now, this is without any time needed or given for recovery on the turns. It appears that the more relaxed you are, the faster you go with less energy required. What prevents extended time swimming in a relaxed state is a little tiredness which creeps upon you, which is down to lack of swimming fitness. Improvement will happen over time and an extended, relaxed style should also come into play.

Still only left side breathing today and feeling comfortable although there is a strong sense of guilt, not forcing myself to try the right side again. There was this irresistible compulsion that I had to do something about, but I knew it would stress me out. These compulsions ultimately were a dare and resisting dares to me is futile. It was out with the kickboard and right side only strokes and breathing next on the agenda. It was effortless and reasonably comfortable with the kickboard, but when the drill reverts to swimming without the kickboard, the confidence and calmness disappear in one fell swoop.

After a while right-side breathing with the kickboard, I further dared myself to do the breathing every three strokes, (bi-lateral) without aids. Before the attempt, I knew it was going to give me grief, causing me to tense up, panic and stop. Why are these dares taken on? True to form, tension built up immediately. It started with losing my count on which side to breathe. After only a couple of metres, I had to skip the breath on the right as I was too scared to take the high risk of water intake. The left side breath always came to the rescue and the length, which was a big struggle, was eventually completed. I was out of breath, but it was another step forward not stopping and my feet firmly seeking refuge on the floor. Another dare will no doubt happen in due course, but not in this session.

Forty-five minutes now under my belt in the pool with many little breaks of bobbing, it was a good feeling knowing that the fear I had before attempting drills was diminishing. Not counting the bi-lateral breathing in front crawl, stopping was rare despite some intake of water on a few occasions but were dealt with while still swimming.

A few manageable breaststroke lengths swam to finish and a good feeling to be back into a three-day a week swim routine.

Amidst this current bright outlook now looms a dark cloud approaching in June. It is now time where the school summer holidays are upon us and all Bulgarian schools close. The swimming pool will also shut down with no swimming facilities in Yambol from June through to the end of September. September 21st is the day of the Serpentine event! Worrying thoughts on where to swim during that time were with me right now.

One Stroke Forward, Two Backwards

I didn't feel like going swimming today. What forced me to go in the end was that I knew if one session missed because I didn't feel like it, others would follow. Being ill and not going is one thing, but not going just because I don't feel like it is another.

It took a real drive against my will to attend this session while carrying out the regular routines in the morning. The rewards for turning up for the session would, however, reflect in achievements made. On the other side of the coin, I wouldn't have had my tail between my legs all weekend feeling guilty, dropped ego and not least no progress made if I hadn't have made an effort.

It was 09:44 at the car park ticket machine and I was feeling much better after the usual 10-minute brisk walk. There was no messing at this point and headway made straight into the pool complex. It was looking and feeling good now, a far cry from earlier.

The pool once entered I found persistently leaking goggles which caused delays in the bobbing and breaststroke warm-up routine. The only remedy known to me was to tighten the strap repeatedly. Only a death-grip hold with constant tightening eventually solved the problem. I knew this probably wasn't normal, but there was no other answer and was looking like another pair of goggles would have to be purchased because of this. Perhaps this time not online, but in a sports shop in one of Bulgaria's bigger cities as I want to try them on before committing to buy. Another option would be to wait for my trip to the UK next month and buy a pair there.

With my head now throbbing from the tightness of the goggles, but no leakage, the warm-up session began. I was bobbing then into breaststroke only doing a few lengths just to get my blood circulating. It was so easy now with this stroke and after ten lengths, it felt like I could go on forever. The only drawback was the time it took to do those ten lengths. The pace was so slow this was a worry. If I use this stroke in the Serpentine swim, I calculate it will take over four hours to complete the 2-mile distance. I see other swimmers easing past me using the same stroke and seemingly the same technique; therefore, it remains a mystery why this is and another reason to work on front crawl. It would give more economy of energy and be worth its weight in gold with speed.

Into the front crawl now with the left side only breathing. I thought I had this cracked over the last two session, but it all went pear-shaped today. Apart from the first length, anxiety and panic returned. No matter how hard I tried to relax and think easy, it didn't make any difference. Once the fear kicked in with water intake, my feet dropped, touching the bottom, which occurred three times in this drill. After only 30 minutes I wanted to leave the pool. However, rather than bow to defeat, I decided to try and fight the temptation to give up. With this additional push to conquer the fear of water intake, each length was now increasingly exhausting with a crumbling technique and failure. I was soon back to where I started a few weeks ago! Not good.

With more frustration in my system and very aware of getting into a whirlpool of tension and anxiety, I talked myself into getting out of the pool and no progress was made today.

With improvements made on the previous two sessions on Monday and Wednesday, it was a stroke backwards today!

On reflection, I assessed today like the proverbial 'bad day at the office'. We all have them and hope that next Monday's session will help me forget today. The front crawl technique is a worry, but I am still very determined to conquer it. The breaststroke was also a worry with the lack of pace.

The session was done throughout with constant pain in my right shoulder; I put up with it. Funny how this type of pain is tolerable, but other uncomfortable and fearful situations (or mental suffering) in the water cannot.

All said and done I won't give up trying to improve, despite the other surrounding problems such as potentially no pool to practice in during the summer.

Comfort Zone Preferred

After a weekend of continuous rain, I was tucked away inside our apartment for the best part of it. With this imprisonment at the weekend, you would think it would be a great temptation this Monday morning after looking out of the window and have pined to get out seeing a glorious sunny rain-free day.

Yes, I couldn't wait to get out being a prisoner of rain for two days, but not looking forward to going swimming, especially after reflecting on what happened in last Friday's session. I have to admit that I don't enjoy swimming, continuously facing up to a 'no comfort zone' most of the time, despite having been working on learning to swim for nearly two months now. It has become a forced event each session and never leaves my head throughout the day and night. Countdowns immediately start up again at the end of each session leading up to a man forcing himself to attend a hostile and foreign environment. Even though my star sign is Cancer, a water sign, it seemingly has no bearing or affiliation for me being akin water.

Once again, I had to force myself to go swimming this morning. Well, at least I will enjoy the walk to the pool if not the swim and of course grateful it's not raining.

It was precisely 09:44 on the car park ticket machine and no time to pause moving into the school swimming complex. After giving the cashier the exact swimming fee, I found that I was the first swimmer into the changing room. The floor was still wet from the mop woman who I passed in the corridor that led up to it.

I usually change my clothes next to a radiator which is generally on - today it wasn't and stone cold. Shame, as it dries my gear once returning after the swim while I get dressed. Old habits die hard as this location in the changing room remains in my domain each time if free - which is most of the time.

This changing room sees many students walking past as there are a gym and a table tennis room next door further along the corridor. It is not private at all when changing clothing. If someone comes in or goes out, leaving the door open, anyone passing can see inside. There is another place with even more indiscretion and for peering eyes manhood revealed - that is in the shower room. If the entrance door is open, there is an unobstructed view of showering men right through the whole length of the corridor which extends past the gym and table tennis room and continues running to the public reception area. Crowds of students and parents linger in the reception area and many students walk along that corridor. My tactic is always to have my back facing the door. That way, all anyone gets to see if they peep is a sight of my bum. That's the least I can do in this situation. It is no big deal as Bulgarian men and women just don't seem to have any scruples about being seen nude, albeit not from the point of being exhibitionists. You only have to see a car parked on the side of public roads for a Bulgarians having a toilet break to realise this – and not only men. No indiscretion gets in the way of a chore or getting on with things and the same applies here.

After a cold shower, it was now getting back trying to enjoy swimming. With some warm-up arm swings and stretching exercises outside the pool, it was into the water and some bobbing drills after adjusting a 'death grip' to my goggles. They still leaked as I took off into the breaststroke warm-up. Having put some more toothpaste on the goggle lenses this morning to avoid fogging, I was determined to try and live with these goggles. Each session that goes by, it appears that leakage gets worse. It ends up having to swim my eyes closed until the end of the length is reached, then stop to empty the water.

Eventually, there was a water-tight seal made, but not before six or seven more tightening adjustments made.

Breaststroke lengths continued as the thought of going into a front crawl and out of the comfort zone didn't appeal. It was a full twenty minutes of breaststroke before I decide to face up to and to get on with other drills. Not knowing how many lengths completed didn't matter, the main positive thing here was that I felt I could have gone on indefinitely with breaststroke. But as before in sessions with breaststroke, the pace is frustratingly slow.

The front crawl was now in line and the aim was just to try and relax and use slow strokes. The challenge was to do three lengths without a break; two lengths had been the norm up until now. I knew that once into the third length, there would be a lot of tensing up and panic. In turn, this would disturb the breathing technique and the swim would fail.

As the routine took me into the third length, my predictions were right. It was almost back to starting all over again with the technique. Trying to push towards the last few metres of that third length was extremely uncomfortable, tense and full of anxiety. It was just like how I used to try and swim before my training started.

Inevitably, the result was me being completely out of breath and stressed something I had been desperately trying to avoid. Right now I just can't see where any extended swimming of more than 50 metres in front crawl can happen. Without a break, how can I get my breath back? The breaststroke option was now menacingly lurking in the background.

More lengths of the front crawl namely two-length bursts which were just about manageable. Thinking back, I remembered that not that long ago, only one length was manageable. From this, there was a little ray of hope ringing out.

The session ended after 40 minutes in the pool. Nearly all of that time was full-blown swimming with only a few bobbing breaks. I could have gone on more, but there was a queue of people wanting to use the pool, so I gave way to them just like the English gentleman I am.

A warm shower at the end and then back home and certainly happier than I was last Friday.

Mind Made Up Then?

Yet again, there was no motivation to go swimming today. With that, I had to force myself to make it happen. There are lots of other things to do and chores waiting in our new acquired village smallholding. With this new farm project, the required work on the land could quite easily distract me and pull me away from attending swimming sessions. The swim is in the mornings usually, which unfortunately coincides with the best time to work on the land as it gets too hot from midday onwards.

Regardless of diversions, it was pacing along the cobblestoned streets of Yambol heading towards the school swimming complex again today. I knew I'd thank myself for making an effort once done. Once the challenge is over, I can't see me swimming anymore unless somehow I was incapable of cycling or running. The reason is simple - I don't enjoy water which seemingly tries its best to drown you. However, what I do get off on is the challenge of trying to face up and conquer these fears and phobias.

Yet again, 09:44 shows on the car parking ticket machine on arrival and straight into the school swimming block. Then only to be told that I have to wait until 10:00 before I can enter. I suspect this was that the receptionist had been told not to let us in early by the woman pool attendant. She prepares the pool checking everything is working and the water is safe before swimmers enter the water. By the time 10:00 came, there were three other swimmers in the reception area waiting with me. Four lanes, four swimmers and looks like we will all have a lane to ourselves.

I was last to change into my swimming outfit purposely not rushing to encourage keeping a calm mental state. The showers were piping hot being the fourth in as I enjoyed the luxury for once. Then onto stretching exercise by the poolside next and into the alien world of water. I intended to just focus on breaststroke at this point. I was now contesting the idea of resigning myself to doing the 2-mile event in breaststroke. I could go on indefinitely with this stroke without even getting out of breath or fatigued. There is not much street cred about it, but it is all about completing the distance no matter how long it takes or how unfashionable it is.

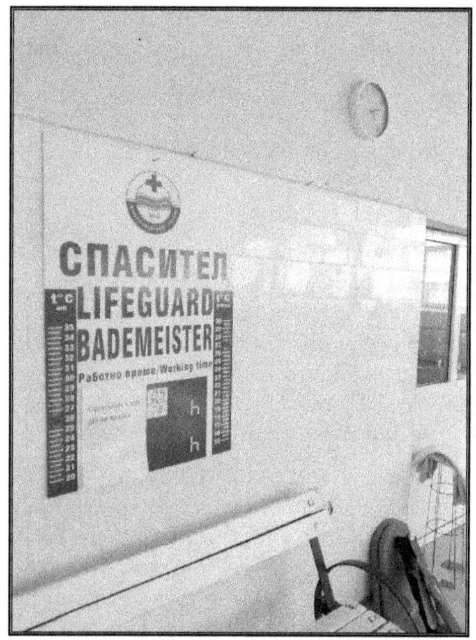

School Pool Clock High up and Water Information

Off I go, up and down, up and down losing count of the lengths completed. After the first ten, I just ploughed on. Easy, easy, easy. Negative thoughts invaded knowing that I wasn't getting any aerobic benefit doing this. At no point were there any stopping or panic situations. There was just one accidental water up the nose, but without any issues, as I stayed calm and brushed the incident aside while still swimming.

I stopped eventually, not from tiredness but just out of curiosity of how long I had been swimming. Being short-sighted I can't see the clock high up on the wall while in the pool. I have to get a near as I can in the pool, raise my goggles and pull my eyelid to the side, making 'slanted eye' impressions to get a little focus on the clock somehow. When I finally got some sharpness in my eye, the clock showed that I had just done a full 35 minutes of non-stop swimming. A feel-good factor hit in straight away.

Just for a little fun, I decided to try the front crawl again with great apprehension. There was a risk that it would deflate me mentally. However, something quite strange happened. I tried to relax and get into a rhythm I could maintain. The focal point here was on stroke style where each arm was waiting for the other to arrive stretched out in front of me before going into another stroke. I also tried to exaggerate turning my body left and right synchronising with each stroke, so there is less effort involved on the arms. Well, the strange thing was I did four lengths non-stop and was only slightly out of breath. I could have easily swum another length, but stopped. The shock of the success caused this and I wanted to reflect as to why this happened.

I couldn't figure it out and went into another two lengths with the same style with the same success. What had clicked here to cause this? Was it because of the significant 35 minutes warm-up with breaststroke beforehand? Was it because I had muesli and a banana for breakfast instead of cheese on toast? Or was it just because I didn't put pressure on myself with high expectations before attempting it?

My intention remains to use breaststroke even with this small miracle happening with the front crawl. I worked out that I would have to complete 188 lengths in this pool to cover the 3200 metres, (2 miles) required. With one minute per length in breaststroke fashion, that works out at just over three hours. I feel at this stage that this is manageable right now.

I will see what happens on Friday's session and probably doing the same as I did today but for longer. Also, there will be some investigations into breaststroke technique online to see if it can be made more efficient.

Second Thoughts on Front Crawl

There was a treat last night watching Arsenal get through to the semi-finals of Football's Europa Cup with a few beers for company. My head didn't hit the pillow until well gone midnight as the match started at 22:00 local time here. (The game was in Italy and Bulgaria is two hours ahead.)

When waking up this morning, it was a tired individual who was subjected to a couple of beer funded toilet trips during the night. Eventually, albeit reluctantly, I swivelled around to land my feet into my slippers by the side of the bed. Ten minutes later and after a good healthy oat-based breakfast and a cup of ginger and lemon tea which prompted some resolute thoughts of the day ahead. I recalled the progress made swimming in the last session and pinned good hope on that continuing. I have to take full advantage of the facilities provided in Yambol while the swimming pool remains open until the school closes for the summer holidays. Finding another venue close to home is going to be difficult if not impossible.

Tracks made to the car park ticket machine which displaying 09:48 on arrival today. I purposely arrived late as I wasn't allowed entry until 10:00 on my last visit. However, no hiccups on entering the pool today, all was ready when I arrived with another swimmer in before me.

Into the swimming gear, a quick shower, then straight into the pool forgetting to do the warm-up stretching before getting into the pool. Trying to do those missed stretching exercised in the water is awkward, especially trying to touch your toes, so I just stopped and got on with the swimming. I just couldn't be bothered with the hassle of getting out of the pool again for stretching routine.

There was a 25 minutes spell of breaststroke working on some techniques seen on a few online tutoring videos. Included in this were bobbing my head up and breathing in after every stroke. Once having given this a go it didn't feel right at all if I had carried on I would have hyperventilated. I think this style is more for sprinters than long-distance swimming, so I gave up on that entirely.

The kicking with legs recommended was a straight kick rather than a frog leg kick style. The kick was done with a slightly splayed leg recovering after the kicking out. It felt strange but seemed to work. It does need to be focused upon all the time as it doesn't come naturally. I tried to work on this throughout the session and will continue beyond this.

The reason I did only 25 minutes breaststroke, (and it was easy) was that there was a particular curiosity lingering in my head. I was thinking about the previous session where after four lengths of front crawl, there was ample breath and energy to spare. Could this happen today again, or was it a one-off? My impatience got the better of me and to satisfy my curiosity; I ended the breaststroke and into the experimental front crawl.

The front crawl was now in progress, as I worked hard, trying to focus on being relaxed and not rush the strokes. The target set was four lengths physiologically knowing that I would have to pace myself with this set goal in place. Towards the end of each length, there is the inevitable rush due to a lure of the turn and break.

By purposely not rushing towards each end, this worked well as I rolled over four lengths with plenty of breath to spare. However, after each length, there was still a noticeable build-up of tension as it progressed with more effort needed to fight each length completed. With this build-up of energy required due to increasing stress, sustaining it over longer distances was impossible. If only I could swim subsequent lengths in the same style of the first length, then I would have cracked it!

Front crawl, therefore, is still something I am still at ill at ease with even though the distance managed without stopping has increased over time. It was only a short time ago I was going to give this stroke up entirely. There was however a nicely nestled ray of hope that set in today. Hope is something that niggles away and that now had seemingly won me over to persevere with front crawl; at least for the time being.

The session continued with three more attempts at four-length durations, all completed. I guess I could have done five lengths but didn't want to go through the motions of getting into the increasing realms of tension that had built up over the first four lengths. It was better to concentrate just trying to relax over the last few of those four lengths for now.

The session finished with a couple of breaststroke lengths, which now I feel quite at home with, but still never to the point where I could say it was enjoyable. Feeling at home but not enjoying breaststroke is perhaps a paradox, but true. It is the lesser of two evils and after all, not everyone is 'happy at home'! All said and done this is something I wouldn't have associated with any kind of swimming a few weeks ago.

Mind Elsewhere Today

I turned up to the pool today with more than a hint of excitement. The 'high' was due to some visible progress made in the last session. However, I found out on arrival that the pool was not open until midday. The President of Bulgaria visiting Yambol was the reason. I did wonder why I saw swarms of traffic police on the roads on the way to the pool. Why would a presidential visit cause the pool to close unless he was visiting the school, which he wasn't? I didn't question as to why as I know things are very different in Bulgaria, much of it without rhyme or reason from an outsider viewpoint. I just walked back home with a little sulk resigned to missing today's session. There was always the next day when people aren't bowing down to the President and unexplained formalities.

So, Monday's session cancelled and now it is Tuesday with 09:46 shown on the car park ticket machine on arrival. First in today the changing room today, but even without company, why was I feeling rushed? For whatever reason, I wanted to get rid of that sense of urgency and purposely took an extended amount of time doing warm-up stretching exercises outside the pool to counteract this.

Today I was determined to try the front crawl with a point of extending the distance in relaxed mode using an effortless built-up style into a 'clockwork' system that I could sustain. The session didn't start too well to my frustration with feet bottoming out after only two lengths of breaststroke. The feet down was in reaction to taking a big gulp of water for reasons I couldn't work out. My mind, however, was also on other things while swimming. Inadvertently multi-tasking with focuses on both swimming technique and other issues outside the field of sport wasn't conducive to progress. With this analysis, I forgave myself on this occasion.

There were four lengths of front crawl managed, but on the last length, the style and technique began to flounder with an ever-growing amount of tension mounting. I knew this would soon lead to panic, so I took a break. Taking breaks with feet on the ground has been the norm until now. Grounding my feet can't happen in London's Serpentine event with deep water.

With this thought, I took it upon myself to try and recover floating on my back as this would be the method used in the event. It worked quite well and helped me get back into a relax mode before starting up again. Morally it helps as well as feet on the ground always gives a sense of failing.

Over the next twenty minutes, it was either two, three or four lengths non-stop front crawl managed. Alongside this, there was either floating on my back method or breaststroke used as recovery sessions. Much would depend on how severe my breathlessness was. During these sessions, I touched the floor just once. This 'one-off' feet grounded annoyed me as I could have easily avoided as it was the result of pure laziness. It was hard concentrating today with distractions outside swimming my head was full of malicious mishmash today.

With things as they were in my head, I didn't enjoy the front crawl at all today. It is all too stressful, especially each time after the first two lengths of swimming. To be quite honest, I couldn't wait for the drills to end. Wanting the session to end leads to trying to speed up and finish sooner and was therefore self-defeating. There wasn't any time when I felt at ease with anything today.

It is still early days and I know the breaststroke with a slow drift would always be there as a safety net. It is only from the point of being bloody-minded that I haven't knocked front crawl on the head by now. There is always that ray of hope lingering that perhaps may grant a little salvation in this area one day. Also, a wetsuit will help with buoyancy and surely this would make the breathing easier with my head and body higher up in the water. Having never worn a wetsuit before, this may be an essential element in June when the school and pool close for summer leaving open waters swimming venues as an option.

The nearest swimming pool to Yambol is around 100 kilometres away. Local open waters that contain giant catfish, snakes along with armed security guards that roam these places weren't too inviting. Most local lakes and other open waters places have corpses of dogs, cats, rats, sheep and the odd human not mention excrement floating down from villages upstream. I have to admit to witnessing most of these in local lakes and rivers while looking for fishing venues locally. Bulgaria, of course, is very different to the UK as I have found out since living here. Also, another challenge altogether was the fact that I know there is a good chance I'd drown attempting open waters right now with deep water and no comfort zone of being able to land my feet on the ground. More confidence is needed in the pool at least while the school pool remains open.

My next session is due in two days on Thursday if all goes to plan. It is Easter this weekend in Bulgaria, so I'm not too sure what the school pool has planned in terms of opening.

Easter Break Is Upon Us

After a night of strange dreams, there was a tasty muesli breakfast to come back to the real world. The usual fresh ginger and lemon tea washed it down and ready for the day ahead.

The weekly plan was shifted forward a day due to the closure of the pool on Monday. It was now Thursday and on course for another session. What's more, this weekend being Easter in Bulgaria after today, the pool is also shut until the following Tuesday so that it will be a 5-day break until the next session.

What I wanted to do today is prove to myself that I had been progressing no matter how small. With this in mind, the challenge was to try and get a five-length non-stop front crawl under my belt. Within this plan, there would be recovery breaks using the floating on your back system included if needed. It was good to practice as it would undoubtedly be used in open water sessions as there are no other options other than sinking underwater.

The Car Park Ticket Machine

It was 09:46 on the car park ticket machine, so far so good. I know what time is going to be shown on the digital clock now, two methods are used to calculate this. The first is knowing what time I leave my apartment and whether I get caught having to wait at the traffic lighted pedestrian crossing. That would take either nine or ten minutes respectfully. Secondly, seeing the regular coach that travels past the school at precisely 09:45 would give the signal and determine whether I an early or late. Today I had to wait for the green light on the pedestrian crossing, so it was one minute added. Also to confirm the one minute delay, the coach passed me 100 metres before reached the school. Instinctively, this is how I accounted for that extra one minute and

I knew it would be 09:46 at the ticket machine before I arrived. There is something quite satisfying, calm and reassuring working these things out. I am, of course, fully aware that this is quintessentially an English phenomenon.

It was second in the pool today with the quest to improve in this session now started. With my mind firmly fixed on the objectives today, I forgot to do the out of the pool warm-up stretching exercises. Once in the pool, however, there was no turning back. I carried regardless with a 20-minute session of breaststroke. Today for some reason, I was sitting lower in the water and naturally, my head sunk lower when expelling air. The techniques on how to get faster in breaststroke remains a complete mystery, regardless of a higher or lower position in the water; I just plodded on. This style is an entirely sustainable swimming action and reassuring that at no time would I get exhausted aerobically, in fact, more bored than fatigued.

Onto the front crawl and quite nervous knowing that the last two lengths of the five-length challenge would very likely bring on panic. With the focus entirely on relaxing and a leisurely pace, by the time the fourth length came about, I wanted to stop, but I forced myself on. Five lengths now under my belt and I was totally and utterly exhausted. I could never understand why, as the slow and unforced strokes used shouldn't exhaust me. The breathing technique is seemingly correctly in place, albeit left side only. The intermittent kicking of the legs just for balance shouldn't tax my lungs, but for some reason, I felt wholly 'knackered' both physically and mentally

After a length of drifting on my back to recover, it was a good time to think. There is no point doing front crawl to exhaustion and it was better to focus on two or three length sessions and recovery on my back until it becomes easier. Then there is always the option to extend the distance later. Also, it is challenging to use breaststroke as a recovery method when completely exhausted from the front crawl. Getting back into the breaststroke when exhausted means I just lose form and tension in this stroke style and panic sets in again.

So the plan now is to swim intermittent front crawl two lengths at a time with floating on the back recovery with an occasional breaststroke length put in if not too exhausted.

This session eventually finished and I went away knowing that the up and coming five-day Easter break would probably do me good. It was going away forgetting about learning how not to drown, then returning for more next Tuesday. There will more than likely be more ballast taken to the pool with me being a few pounds heavier. This weight gain is if you haven't already guessed would be from the Easter feasting and celebrations that traditionally on here.

Breaststroke - Why is it so Easy?

Easter celebrations and feasting over and the high school reopens, which meant the swimming pool is also back in business. It is now 'actions stations' all over again.

Today I didn't feel like going swimming and was trying to think of a viable excuse not to go. No matter what I thought up, it didn't come anywhere near to qualifying as a valid reason for skipping. Having got stung by a bee over the weekend, which caused a swollen right arm was the main argument contested for not going. That original reason used as ammunition for an excuse ironically turned out to be an incentive and motivated me to go. Training with a 'disability' is another challenge with the vision of myself becoming a self-proclaimed macho hero. However, in others' eyes here in Bulgaria, I would be seen as an English fool. Their reasoning as to why do some people purposely force themselves, putting themselves through these pain barriers is justified. Of course, this is seen by natives here as typically English eccentric fad.

There was another escape route from the session from Galia. She had a job interview at 10:30 this morning. She didn't want me to fuss over her, but I'm here to help and it was difficult for me not to. From Galia's point of view, it was probably better for me to be somewhere else rather than waiting for the result nervously; we agreed! Besides, I would just be a hindrance with over-helpfulness, lingering and giving Galia constant reassurance. It would be better for all to go and focus on something more practical such as swimming rather than having a workout in thumb-twiddling.

Decision made and it 09:44 showing on the car park ticket machine and without hesitation the short tramp into the school pool block. The playground was like an assault course. Trying to avoid basketballs and footballs that were being thrown and kicked at random from happy sporting students out in the warm spring Bulgarian sunshine was a bit of fun.

I didn't have a plan today other than just to try and enjoy the swim. Sadly, enjoyment had been missing from swimming from the very start of the training back in March. It was impossible to enjoy with the numerous occasions of frustrations trying to master the front crawl stroke. There was an unquenchable drive within me to push further to avoid the self-humiliation of failure with this discipline. The focus was so intense once off the mark I forgot to do the warm-up stretching exercises before entering the pool – and not the first time!

I was now in the water and something I didn't forecast came about. Initially, I was expecting a struggle with a grimace to conquer the painful bee-stung swollen arm. However, to my surprise, the water was an excellent remedy and soothed the pain in my right arm. With this relief and easing of pain, there was no distraction for the swimming drill and disciplines planned.

Breaststroke strokes began as I noted the time at 09:55 on the wall clock. There were gentle and smooth strokes and shallow breathing every two strokes. It felt good so far, although so very obvious that the pace was slow. Each time I looked at the progress being made by looking down at the line at the bottom of the pool lane pass under me, it was as if it moved in slow motion. This lack of pace used to be a big concern, but the effort made involved slow was next to nothing. This swimming style could be sustained forever in my mind.

After around eight lengths, I lost count and just carried on. It was so comfortable I could have fallen asleep during this drill. There were a few occasions where my eyes closed just to relieve the boredom and play with guessing the swimming direction taken blind.

The breaststroke just kept going on and on as I was in a well-earned comfort zone from learning curves made. The further it went on, the bigger the thoughts became of neglecting the front crawl. However, this made me feel guilty regardless of the knowledge that I wouldn't enjoy any other stroke, so for the meantime, I ploughed on. It felt selfish with this stance given my resolve to improve my freestyle, but what the hell for now.

Pushing with my legs against the wall to start each length felt like it was cheating. There is a distance gained with this which would not happen in open waters. Therefore, I purposely start in a still position and started to move off with the sole use of my arms. Now, I avoid any temptation to propel myself off the wall with a leg push.

I knew there would be times where the swim will have to pause. The break was for either emptying water that has entered into goggles or water up the nose or sneezing. I had to sneeze in the pool today as I turned onto my back, made the sneeze then rolled back over and continued. Dealing with this event was very rewarding being able to do this, plus the fact that it would be more comfortable in a wetsuit with the aid a trailing tow float if needed. Reassurance comes to mind knowing these tools of the trade will be with me.

As time moved on the pool had more visitors, including children who now wanted to share my lane. I had no idea how long I had been swimming non-stop. My breaststroke takes up the whole of the lane and often my hand hits the wall or more frequently the two water filters that stick out as I pass them. With the sharing of a lane, it would become even more obstructive, so at this point, I decided to stop.

A look at the clock which I could just make out with my goggles up and stretching my eyelids side-wards, it was 10:45. I had been swimming non-stop for 50 minutes. This lengthy swim was a big surprise, especially as there was no fatigue or out of breath throughout that swim. Working the mileage out, I had done around 850 metres. To me, that was amazing! Three thousand two hundred metres required in the Serpentine event was now something I felt I could have probably managed today, albeit pool metres, not open water metres.

I finished off with three lengths of front crawl just to remind myself how uncomfortable it is. And it was!

Now here was a dilemma. Do I work on duration in breaststroke or persevere with front crawl? Front crawl in my mind is the challenge, so my mind is made up. Breaststroke for me it too easy and doesn't set up any real demands physically. In the back of my mind, of course, is the knowledge that I am capable of completing the 2-mile swim with breaststroke if needed.

So glad I went swimming today and my bee-stung right arm is now feeling much better from an hour of being soothed in mild waters.

Chapter 4 (May)

Training Idea Taken On

Bee stings are becoming a regular trait here on the farm as I was stung again, this time on my right ear. Regardless of not being able to sleep not being lying on my right side, the show still goes on with the swimming. To prevent stings from happening again, I bought myself a beekeeper's hat. There had been no more encounters of the bees that give me grief with impaling me with their poison weapons to date - fingers crossed.

Beekeeper's Hat On

Aggressive bees aside, I was given some training advice from two kind acquaintances online on a sporting community site called RealBuzz.com. They knew the issues I have with front crawl and also are aware of my comfort zone in breaststroke. Their suggestion was to use alternate the strokes styles and just use breaststroke as a recovery. I was doing this before, but never purposely focused on in that way.

It was a sunny warm day and I was looking forward to the walk to the pool in the radiant heat. No jeans today as I donned a pair of shorts. It is strange, but I always feel a kind of liberated wearing scant clothing. With this, I count myself fortunate getting the chance to wear such fashion during the long Bulgarian summers. The other perk with limited dressing, there is less work in the changing rooms with less clothing to change and hang up.

Today's time was 09:46 when I arrived at the car park ticket machine and subsequently, the second person in the pool. This time it was a relaxed feeling as I did the stretching exercises before entering the pool. I had lost count how many times I forget to do these on previous occasions.

Four lengths of easy breaststroke take off for the warm-up. Front crawl then kicked in whenever I felt up to it and as the session moved on this became more frequent. Initially, it was only one length of front crawl and two of breaststroke then upped to two of each later in the session. Sometimes there was an issue of losing form when reverting to breaststroke due to exhaustion and on one occasion I had to roll over and recovered drifting on my back for a few moments. Far better than the previous breaks with feet down.

This constructive drill continued throughout the session. The next thing I knew, I'd been swimming non-stop for 55 minutes. I must have covered well over one kilometre during that time and still had loads of energy left at the end of it.

The shower and changing back into my clothes was sweet with the thought of the success shown today. Taking the advice given by the two kind and caring ladies worked. I guess it just takes a third party to tell you rather than being left to my ineptitude of self-taught training.

I now look forward to the next training session with a sense of eagerness to build on what I did today. And I hoped for no more bee stings with my new beekeeper hat once I'd arrive to work on the farm after the swim.

Just As Things Were Going Well!

It was Tuesday today, not Monday where my usual planned swimming session takes place and this was for a good reason.

Monday the 6th May was St George's Day in Bulgaria which celebrates all people given the name George or variant of that name and Galia included in that group. The day was also one of a celebration of the Bulgarian National Armed Services and marked as a national holiday. That means festive parties, traditional gatherings with no work and school closed, which means no swimming pool open.

The pool closed was the first disappointment, although there is always tomorrow to play catch up. I had chores on the land before the storms that are forecast come in later that day. I was the only one working on this national holiday, but then I'm English and find it hard to follow the culture of leaving jobs that need doing on days like this.

The second disappointment after a morning on the farm was spending the whole afternoon on my laptop intending to purchase a wetsuit. My goodness, they are so expensive! Even renting one out is well over my budget on my small pension here. Some from China is cheaper, but from what I read, they aren't durable therefore not suitable for swimming and designed for other water-based sports such as sailing or surfing. However, I may have to opt for one of these regardless as the price is bearable. From experience though, I know that dirt-cheap wetsuits from China would be a false economy, just like the goggles I bought earlier in the year. I don't have enough fingers and thumbs to count the number of other times I've regretted purchasing cheap far eastern products online. Will I learn from this or submit to the temptation of frugality?

We had an evening of celebration in the name of St George. Our 'George Name Day' was based in a restaurant that evening with my partner and her son. (Eating in restaurants is a rare event for us I might add.) Not a lot to drink, just one rakia with a salad, one bottle of Bulgarian beer and a pizza. Afterwards, we took a pleasant 15-minute walk home in the dark of the night passing through the beautifully lit city centre radiated from solar-powered lighting. By the way, the storms that were forecast didn't arrive much to my disappointment. There is nothing like a good storm to clear the air. The farmland also needed a proper watering and it didn't happen. It's also a good feeling when rain arrives to save on electric that is required to pump water up from the deep well.

The third disappointment today was finding out that there are no safe open water venues locally for swimming. There have been occasions where I see places that we pass by that seemingly look suitable, so it was a shock to hear this. I was warned by locals each time I questioned the suitability of waters and told each time that they that are severely polluted. Every year many gipsies end up at the bottom of these lakes and rivers, but not reported. Everyone I speak to on this topic has the same opinion that if I don't die from drowning, it will be from poisoning from contaminated waters or shotgun wounds from security wardens. They also mentioned the snakes and massive catfish that live in these waters and stories of attacks are frequent.

Having first arrived in Bulgarian some 14 years ago, I do not doubt what people tell me about the waters around here. Even in the mid-summer with sweltering temperatures, I don't recall seeing anyone swimming in open waters before. The only sights I see of bathing in these waters are gipsy youths in very shallow waters, but never venturing into deep sections.

Scenic Open Waters in Yambol, but Polluted

All set up for today with toothpaste smeared goggles and swimming kit prepared kit meticulously set up in my shoulder bag. It was the first time for a long time that I was looking forward to the session. Even with thoughts of no open swimming opportunities and the closure of the pool for three months during the school summer break, I was feeling optimistic.

A storm finally did arrive early this morning. The walk to the pool involved me trying to avoid numerous rain-filled pools in the roads and pavements. With this puddle dodging walk, it was a 09:47 arrival time on the car park ticket machine. The lateness compounded by intermittent stops having to sort out my brolly in strong swirling winds, but no matter.

My head turned away from the car park ticket machine and I saw a sight that wasn't normal in the routine leading up to the swimming session. Sometimes noticing just one thing in an instance creates an oracle as to what to expect next. My observations gave rise to a man walking into the school entrance. That may seem entirely innocent, but I knew this man wasn't a teacher. A much-enjoyed pastime of mine is watching people; I do it all the time trying to work out what type of person I am looking at with their dress sense body language and other mannerisms. I knew instinctively by observing this man he was alien to the surrounding environment. He had a weather-beaten face, a hat that looked like it had been pressed on his head looking like a Victorian sponge cake powdered with icing sugar. His mannerisms included a walk that staggered and weaved as if he wasn't quite sure where to go. There was no reaction from him to the students that were swarming around as he continued his ramble.

To me, this man was here for maintenance or more likely repair with his dust-covered clothing. As I followed him in, my heart sank. I knew my analysis of this man was indeed correct. I saw a yellow builders' truck outside the entrance to the pool building. Also, there was a pipe in the back of the work truck. This pipe had been rolled out into the entrance door and beyond and I instinctively knew the pool would not be open having seen this.

I entered the building and the receptionist cubical was bare and locked up. The pipe that had entered the building extended through another door which led into the pool area. A worker was standing by the door. I asked him what was going on, but I already knew what the answer would be. He stated the obvious saying that the pool was under repair. He then led me to the open main entrance door. He shut the door and showed me a sign that I didn't see due being hidden with the door being ajar. It stated that repair work to the pool would be from the period 7th May to 23rd May - I was in complete dismay!

I don't have a tail, but it was a walk home with one trailing between my legs. I wouldn't be able to train as there is no pool until the 23rd May. Added to this was the planned visit to see my kids in the UK from the 22nd May to 31st May. I knew now that for the whole of May there would be no opportunity to swim. With no open waters to practice, this left me with a big dilemma.

There was a lot of thinking going on now.

A Bigger Challenge Now

It had been ten days to date with no opportunity to swim. The local school swimming pool is next available on Monday 3rd June after repairs.

Will one month without a swim be a problem? What happens after the schools shut up for the summer break in a few weeks? There's no chance of forgetting how to swim, but without building up endurance and work to improved technique will this be a big step backwards?

Open water swimming here in Bulgaria is something that still plagued my mind; should I be taking a chance? Despite everyone lecturing about the dangers whenever I mention the idea, it puts a new quest in front of me. And who isn't up for challenges? With Galia working six days a week, swimming in open waters would have to be on my own without her supervision. Going solo is a worry if I get into difficulty and here there is no Thunderbirds International Rescue.

The Black Sea – Just Over an Hour Away

What are the options if no pool or open waters are available for me right up to the Serpentine event in September? Well, that would be the biggest challenge to date by completing the swim without any training for five months! If the event was today, I know the 2-miles distance would be difficult. Challenging yes, but I was quite confident that I could complete it, albeit at a snail's pace. With occasional pauses and a tow float using breaststroke would get me through. Sporadic stretches could be done in front crawl to speed up a bit but would be short-lived. Having thought about this, it was on the term of doing the event today. But the swim is in September a further four calendar months down the line.

For now, I had come to terms with no swimming until 3rd June. I planned to hunt opportunities in the UK while visiting my children next week. During those nine days in the UK, I will also be purchasing a wetsuit and float tow online to save on the postage costs to Bulgaria. These will be brought back with me to Bulgaria and possibly launched into open waters here. There was the possibility of a day trip to the Black Sea on occasional Sundays when Galia has a day off work. The Black Sea is only some 100 kilometres away from our home; just over an hour away. We've done that before, so why not again?

I am not giving up because of the lack of facilities. That would be too easy and an easy escape route for someone who wasn't so bloody-minded about getting a medal. With the trouble I have had entering the event, it wouldn't serve my mind right to leave the quest behind now.

There was still weight training continuing three times a week and wads of work on the farmland which at least benefits muscles and gives aerobic workouts. No time for bike riding though. Usually, this would concern me, but as I have found out, it doesn't provide any benefits concerning the disciplines of swimming so that I can live with that for now.

The month of May is now a redundant month for swimming without waters. I look forward to returning from the UK with dividing rod to hand perhaps searching for waters to swim in the meantime.

Brainstorming Plans

Being resigned with no swimming during the whole of May due to lack of facilities, my mind was preoccupied with preparing training plans set out for June and beyond.

I took up suggestions from friends on RealBuzz.com and wrote to the Bulgarian Swimming Federation asking them is there are facilities for swimming in my area. However knowing Bulgaria pretty well now, I knew they either wouldn't answer or come up with an impractical suggestion such as a move to a bigger city or use the Black Sea. I am not pessimistic, but I am a realist and generally know how Bulgarians think and act in these matters. Because of this, I don't expect any results from my correspondence.

I tried to entice a reply with the offer of doing the event for a Bulgarian charity. Swimming for charity was pencilled into my original plans anyway, but I fear this call will fall on deaf ears. It had been six days since this email was sent and up to now no response as predicted.

Here in Bulgaria they just don't have the financial clout to conjure up public swimming pools in all towns and cities. In Yambol where I live, it is technically a city but has no public swimming pool, which might surprise those in more affluent Western Europe zones. A European city or town without public swimming baths!?. Opening the school swimming pool to the general public was an enterprise to help maintain the pool with the funds which began two years ago. I was fortunate that this happened as without it, learning to swim would not have been possible and I only entered the London Serpentine event because of this facility.

Here is the email message sent to the Bulgarian Swimming Federation:

Dear Sir/ Madam,

Firstly may I introduce myself as a retired English expatriate living with my Bulgarian partner in Yambol since 2005.

Earlier this year, I decided to enter a charity two-mile open water swimming event that takes place in the Serpentine Lake in Hyde Park, London, in September 2020. (https://www.swimserpentine.co.uk/) I started training for this event in March after being lucky enough finding a local swimming pool to train.

I currently use the swimming pool based in the Mathematical High School 'Atanas Radev'. The staff in the school have been very kind and accommodating since I started knowing that I was a beginner. As far as I am aware, this is the only swimming pool in Yambol. My problem is that once the summer holiday break starts for schools, the pool closes and I am faced not being able to train for a two-mile open water event taking place in September in London.

As you have the expertise and knowledge of the swimming fraternity and infrastructure in Bulgaria, I ask for help to find any swimming venues I can practice in locally. At the same time, the school and the pool close. If there are no pools locally, then, open waters venues are a viable option. With the two-mile event in open waters, any areas of

With only four months to go to the event, it has to be open water training from June onwards. Warnings of the dangers involved aside and I will return from the UK on the 31st May armed with a wetsuit and tow float. Then it may be just a dive into a local reservoir after a trial run with the wetsuit in the school pool. The pool should have re-opened by after repairs by this time. I do also have in mind that the pool shuts again for the summer break shortly afterwards.

Having said all this with a degree of enthusiasm, I still don't enjoy swimming. Strangely, I can't wait to get into the water again even with this personal pet hate of water and the sport. The drive is purely from a fear of not being able to complete the event in September due to lack of practice. In a sense, failure to compete is not an option as it would be bad for my mental health and ego.

While in the UK with swimming trunks packed, I will try and source a public swimming pool there. I know pools are there and but expensive, which may well put me off. Who knows though, maybe I might get a few session in some open waters with supervision from family there if the wetsuit and tow float is in my hands.

Tools for the Trade Now In Hand

I was in the UK for nine days visiting my three sons, daughter and granddaughter, which is excellent as I haven't seen them for well over two years.

One of the first jobs on the swimming front was to find and order a wetsuit and tow float. With plenty of solo time on my hands during the stay as they are all at work most days, this could happen.

Taking part in an auction on eBay, I ended up winning a decent second-hand Blueseventy Reaction triathlon wetsuit for £75. I had to ask the seller to send it first class as there was a risk of it turning up here after I had left. The seller, (a triathlon competitor) couldn't do enough to get it to me as soon as possible after hearing my story. It was a good feeling to find such comradeship in this instance. This, from my experience, happens with many who have a common sporting interest, especially in the amateur field.

The wetsuit turned up on the doorstep the very next day. It was a sense of great nervousness opening the parcel and seeing the outfit. Having never touched a wetsuit, let alone wear one before, I was very hesitant to try it on without looking advice online. The decision I made was to wait until my return home to Yambol before poking my arms and legs in and zipping myself up.

Later on, the same day my tow float arrived, this was ordered from Wiggle. I had used this company before in the UK when buying cycling equipment. The model was a DHB safety buoy and bag. I felt that a big float was a necessary assurance that there was something substantial to cling to at any time of panic in the water.

With the original intention of finding a swimming pool here, this just fell off the end. If the truth is known, I have to own up of not really wanting to spend a fortune on the travel and then expensive pool fees. To put that cost in perspective, the price of bus and an hour in the public swimming pool would be the same as a week's budget on food and drink for us in Bulgaria. It now, therefore, remains for me to get back home and start up swimming again in the more familiar and affordable territory.

While here in the UK, I felt like a stranger with uneasy feelings when treading the streets. Even though I had lived and worked in West Yorkshire for thirteen years, I couldn't recapture any sense of a homecoming.

My fitness topped up with my stay in the UK by landscaping my son's garden during my long lonely moments during the working week. Lots of digging, weeding out aggressive brambles, stubborn old shrubs and rocks, raking and laying a patio area stones took place. I lost at least two kilograms in weight during that time with my heart resting rate down to around 50 beats per minute by the end of my stay.

My son has a road bike with a seized front brake. There was a great temptation to sort that problem out and go cycling. That didn't happen whist the garden project was in full swing due to lack of time. Once the garden project had finished, there were two days left to go and there was still time to get some cycling in; however, it rained the whole of that time. Besides, I would have had to buy work tools for the bike to get it serviceable as there were none here at my son's home. You can tell he's not a keen cyclist, but probably would be if he was living with me! I did ask him whether he wanted to do the swim with me in London. He was reluctant saying he suffers from panic attacks in the water just like me and he was too young to die; unlike me! Shame, it would have been great to have my son as a companion with the swimming challenge.

It remains now that I am determined to try and get some open water swims back in Bulgaria with the wetsuit and tow float to hand. The beauty of open water swimming is that it is free, albeit, dangerous and foolhardy in others' eyes. If I look and search hard enough, I might find a suitable place. As mentioned before, there is always the sea to swim in. My flight back to Bulgaria lands in Burgas airport situated only a five-minute walk to the shoreline of the Black Sea. Conceivably I could try out the wetsuit there on my return. I get to Bulgaria at around 10:30 on Friday. Having left the UK at 22:30 the previous night, I knew there would have been no sleep all night with this disjointed journey. Tiredness, therefore, would play a significant factor in with this plan, although perhaps adrenalin might overcome that.

The Bulgarian Swimming Federation – No Help at all!

There was still nothing from the Bulgarian Swimming Federation in response to my email I sent them a few weeks ago. This non-response was just as expected and now I have to take matters into my own hands finding alternative water venues. Might be surprised with a hunt now on once back home.

With four months to go to the event there is ample time to push a bit more with endurance on the front crawl style and use breaststroke as a recovery stroke. It worked well before the school pool shut down for repairs back in April. However, one whole month without swimming feels like a lifetime, I just hope I can pick things up close to where I left off.

Chapter 5 (June)

The Return to Waters

No open water swimming was taken up in the UK even though my wetsuit and float tow had both arrived safely there. Deciding not to try the wetsuit on, working on the garden project and seeing my family again, swimming effectively just took a back seat the whole time I was there.

Having left the UK late evening, I arrived back home in Yambol at around 11:00 the following day with no chance of me sleeping throughout that time. I can't sleep on planes, trains or for that matter the airport benches. The plan was to go swimming the following Monday on the 3rd June knowing that the pool in the school would now probably be open for business again. Restarting training would be the first swim for six weeks! However, even with this length of time out of the water, there was an issue. This problem would prolong the non-swimming time even further.

Back in my village farm, there was an arrangement for someone to look after the place on my absence. When I turned up at the farm, I was shocked and dismayed to see that my farm had turned into a jungle. Many of my planted produce had died due to lack of watering in the sweltering heat Bulgaria had throughout my time away. It was now a quest to save my crops somehow. Working full-time with the salvage operation, that week following the return from the UK did not allow any time for swimming.

After the week of hard labour on the farm, things were pretty much back to where they should be. There was lots of replanting, saving what I could and not least, the primary task of back-breaking weeding. Ten days in the height of the growing season without any man-management around is something that I won't allow to happen again.

Now things were back to normal, all was ready for a swim the following Monday. I turned up at the car park ticket machine dead on 09:45. As I entered the block, a teacher approached me and explained that there would be loads of kids in the pool shortly. He went on to say that it would be better to come back after 4 o'clock. I was now fully committed mentally to swim and didn't want any more delays. I thanked him for the advice but went straight into the changing room to carry on with my quest for a swim regardless. It was going through the old routines and indeed remembering the warm-up exercises before entering into the pool.

A relaxed breaststroke was the plan for the whole session, having not swum for over six weeks. As warned, children came swarming into the pool after around 10 minutes and I moved my swim into the furthest lane away to try and avoid them. Throughout the session, my lane was avoided by children on the adult trainer's instructions, so in the end, thankfully, it wasn't a problem at all.

Farm Back to Normal after a Week of Hard Labour

After about 30 minutes of non-stop breaststroke and feeling surprisingly good, I popped in the occasional front crawl. Not entirely comfortable with this, but carried on working on alternate two lengths of breaststroke and one front crawl for the remainder of the time in the pool. The time in the water swimming without a break was around 45 minutes. I could have easily gone on well beyond that time.

After the swim, it was a big pleasant surprise to me feeling so good after that length of time away from water. I wasn't bothered about front crawl too much right now as know the event is achievable without it. However, I will pursue with the front crawl technique as I go along. All that labouring in the landscaping in the UK and on the farm back home must have benefitted and increased fitness levels.

I wasn't sure how long the school remains open and many students are already in a party mood with the school year close to ending. I needed no reminding that the pool will close after that.

I had made inquiries into the use of local lakes, rivers and fishing venues. Again I was warned off big time from other people when I asked about swimming in these places. I was also told by countless people that I wouldn't be a welcome party in the fishing venues and many other local waters that prohibits public use. There is armed security in these places and they wouldn't hesitate to shoot trespassers. They also joked that I would be an easy target with a bright orange tow float! Once again, mentions of potentially dangerous waters including pollution, wild animal predators and armed security guards are swarming around most of our local rivers, lakes and reservoirs.

No venues for swimming remained a big issue. With the sea as a last-ditch option, the distance, cost and time involved during the height the holiday season may restrict or even curtail that option.

In Waters Again

I turned up to the school pool two days later on Wednesday 12th June at precisely 09:45 then only to see crowds of children and their mothers queuing up at the reception area. I knew what the instructions would be, namely to turn up after 16:00 so I didn't bother joining the queue. Having been put off having to dodge kids in the pool, even after 16:00, I decided to try again two days later on Friday - probably in vain.

Two days had passed as I arrived at the school intending to swim. I was allowed in at 09:45 with only a scattering of kids seen on my arrival. So it was back in the water in earnest trying to get some form of training which has been scarce over the last couple of months. All I planned was to repeat previous drills of up and down length after length with breaststroke and while this was ongoing try to get some sporadic front crawl in. Then back to breaststroke each time to recover and get my breath back.

The plan worked well, although the maximum I can manage at this point in front crawl was four or five lengths. From this point, the fatigue had built up, causing the swimming style and breathing technique going to pot. I'm sure this is due to lack of regular swims, but nothing I can do as it is totally out of my control. At the back of my mind was thoughts of breaststroke and the tow float as a saviour to complete the 2-miles; even though I have not tried it out yet.

I had been swimming for about 20 minutes and suddenly a flood of children entered the pool area. They were in various age groups with numerous swimming instructors and assistants. Over the next 5 minutes, I had to change lanes three times to avoid a getting swarmed. With this chopping and changing lanes, there was no chance of getting any regular pattern of repetitions in my planned drills. I kept going but finally gave up after another further 10 minutes of more lane hopping. It seemed as if they didn't want me there and fair due, after all, it is a school swimming pool built for students!

I left wondering when the next swim was going to happen, if at all once the school shuts. Sea swimming in salty water isn't the same as freshwater swimming as it is in the Serpentine Lake.

The pondering goes on.

Chapter 6 (July)

Sea Swimming

It was a well-deserved trip to the Black Sea that we both needed. Galia hadn't had a break since starting up work again back in May and I hadn't swum for a few weeks. With Galia having just Sundays off each week, we decided to leave for the coast late Saturday afternoon after she finished work. The Saturday evening journey meant that we could stay there for two nights, then return to Yambol early Monday morning well in time for her to start work. Luckily for us, we could do this as the drive is only an hour and twenty minutes away with my steady driving.

First Time in a Wetsuit

So that's what we did. The plan for me was to try out the wetsuit, which I just manage to squeeze into for the first time with difficulty the night before. It was a tight fit, but once on, it felt quite comfortable, albeit suffering somewhat with sweltering heat it causes. The temperatures here are bordering 30C and above every day during the summer months. Summer days here are something a wetsuit is certainly not suited for. It feels more like a 'sweatsuit' than a wetsuit!

We packed up and happily drove off, looking forward to the break and sea activities.

We stayed at a place called Pomorie, famous for its therapeutic mud that lies on the shore of Pomorie Bay. There are the renowned salt plains and salt museum there right next to the free public accessible 'mudlark' area. The bay where the mud sits seems a perfect place for open water swimming. A bay brings about waters that are calm without currents with a track parallel along the curved line of the coast. However, the temptation being smothering with the therapeutic mud for our aches and pains took precedent and the wetsuit and tow float remained unpacked. We had done this many times with the mud or to a layman's eye, 'muck' before, so we knew how good this treat was for us.

There was however some swimming to made in these waters. It was a pleasant shock when I found that the front crawl style seemed surprisingly easy in these saltwaters. Swimming in seawater where your body rises high with the salt content made the breathing so much more comfortable. With my head now a few more centimetres above the water line each time I swivel to the side for breath, it was a confidence booster. After only a short swim, which rinsed the clinging mud off my body, I felt that could have swum freestyle all day long in these waters.

On Sunday, we visited the main Pomorie Beach full of sand and void of dark grey mud. There was over an hour of swimming that took place in total, which saw me swim from one buoy to another. All the buoys are equidistance to each other and each time one was reached it felt like a small goal achieved.

This swimming session used effortless breaststroke used with intermittent front crawl. It was more difficult breathing with waves hitting me from the side and with only having the left side for my breath in my proverbial locker put me at a disadvantage. I could see now the privilege of bilateral breathing and therefore, should still need working on. No wetsuit (or tow float) used here, mainly because the weather was far too hot standing at well over 30C. I might have considered the wetsuit if we made it to the beach earlier, say 07:00 with much cooler temperatures. All said and done I managed well without a wetsuit. A tow float for me would be an essential part of the kit used in sea swimming which I will try out at some point. With this, it would lead me to have more confidence to go out further to sea.

It remains that I'll have to try out the wetsuit another time just to find out how it feels in the water.

At least there was some swimming here and Galia had deserved a break as we returned to Yambol as planned Monday morning. We were both revitalised with the mud treatment and certainly refreshed mentally after a few days away.

Galia and I Couldn't Resist the Pomorie Mud

Birthday Swim - Regardless

Today was my 61st birthday and I was determined to pursue my quest for a swim with the event fast approaching in September. Oh my God, it's just over seven weeks away!

I turned up at the school pool just after 14:00. As I approached, there was the sound of children echoing from the pool arena. As it was my birthday, it is the tradition here in Bulgaria for the Birthday person to hand out chocolates or treats to friends, family and acquaintances. So I was duly armed with a box of chocolates and presented the treats to the receptionist. She gave me the standard congratulations and good wishes which included good health, luck and success over the coming year. I feel she didn't have the heart to refuse me entry given the kids swarming the place. So seemingly the chocolate signature on my birthday did the trick for a swim.

There was, however, another big surprise on my birthday; the pool will remain open throughout the summer. Furthermore, I can use it from August 1st without the brigades of children as they will be on their summer holiday breaks. The school pool was originally going to close for repairs over the summer break. The conversation revealed that the repairs made a couple of months ago had finished earlier than planned; as documented in earlier chapters. Therefore, no remedial work needed during the summer vacation period.

This information was such a relief to hear and vital for my quest in this 2-mile challenge. Stress levels took a sudden dip and the celebrations in my head went far higher than plain old birthday elations. I suddenly realised how much stress with the preoccupation 'no pool in the summer' worries, for what had seemed like an eternity. The thought of nowhere to swim during the summer months is now over. It was such an enlightening moment to have that dark cloud raised.

How much suffering would I have to go through taking part in the 2-mile swimming event without a swim for three months? I intended to complete the swimming event come what may. Regardless of preparation, lack of training venues and proper equipment, I was ready to suffer for the cause.

However, this now gives a 6-week window from the August 1st to September 20th to get some endurance swimming in regularly. Open water swimming will be restricted only in sea waters as there are still no avenues in other open water areas elsewhere. And why should I risk swimming in life-threatening polluted waters when there are other options now?

While in the changing rooms getting kitted out for the swim, there was a crowd of children gossiping; the box of chocolates came out again. I gave them out to around to half a dozen children who in turn individually wished me a happy birthday. None of the children refused the treat and every single one gave me a sincere birthday greeting in exchange the gift of chocolate.

The Birthday swim in my head now turned into a 'swim for fun' and a 'try to enjoy it' session. Lane hopping, bumping into kids and various other collision avoidance tactics took place throughout the course. The commotion didn't bother me in the least now as I was now thinking ahead to clutter-free waters from the August 1st. Regardless of what misdemeanours the children got up to in the water trying their hardest and disrupt my swimming routine, it didn't matter one bit today!

August 1st is where the real training will start. Perhaps I might get to enjoy swimming in the event with the opportunity of some decent preparation, although six weeks isn't a long time. The final week I will take it easy and wind the intensity down for the big day.

The use of the school swimming pool during the summer break, which was a bleak outlook until today was a wonderful birthday present!

Wetsuit Tried Out in Sea Waters

It was Sunday which meant it was Galia's only day off from work. Sunny, hot weather was here with us alongside Galia's daughter-in-law and grandson who had pleaded for a day trip to the Black Sea with us.

There was no hesitation from me as I prepared to drive us all to the beach, but I did it with one condition tied in which was to leave early and get on the beach before 09:00, so I can try out the wetsuit. It now meant that we should have a choice of prime positions on the beach and it wouldn't be too hot as the forecast was for 34C by midday.

We left at 07:00 sharp and arrived as a coastal village called Sarafovo, right next to Burgas Airport. We have been there many times before as it still retains a seaside village atmosphere. It is overlooked by many tourists who make a beeline for more popular touristy resorts north and south of this location. With this remaining a little secret seaside village it still has a big appeal to us while it lasts.

We arrived and were set up on the beach by 08:30. The ladies and three-year-old child (his first visit to the beach) were all relaxed and enjoyed the sun, sea and sand with a few beers alongside. I, however, had another plan and out of curiosity couldn't wait to get into the waters donning a wetsuit for the first time.

The wetsuit dressing up technique taken on was to use plastic bags to help ride up the legging and arms. This method is the only way making it possible to get into it without ripping the material with force needed to move it along sweating skin. Without this aid, I don't know how anyone can get into a wetsuit without ruining it.

The temperature had already risen to 30C and by the time I had got the wetsuit up to my waist, I was now sweating like a pig. This making it even harder to get the wetsuit skin to ride up, even with the aid of plastic bags.

Issues continued as there was no way I could zip the suit up at the back on my own. The partings at the back needed to be pulled and stretched towards each other to give a little slack enabling the zip to ride up.

It took a while but with female help, the wetsuit was finally on and sealed up. I decided not to use the tow float just yet as I just wanted to get the feel of the wetsuit. Not surprisingly, I was the only person on the beach dressed up looking like a seal but felt nice to be different and individual.

Sarafovo – A 10-Minute Walk from Burgas Airport

The sea temperature was around 26C, but even in seemingly warm water, I saw many people cringe entering with the water once went above the waistline. The first thing I noticed was no sensation of change of temperature on my body as I wade into waters up to my neck. I was more than impressed with the insulation properties of this suit. That was a major surprise as to how effective it was and if this works in much colder waters, this would be a godsend.

As I began to try and swim breaststroke, it was a shock to find out that I couldn't. My legs rose so high when I kicked it was the air I was kicking not water with no propulsion at all. With my legs forced up, this meant my front end was now counterbalanced and forced down. With this, I had to use more energy with my arms to propel my head up for breathing. It felt very uncomfortable trying to get any forward movement with this kit on. Even after 10 minutes of trying to adapt and experimenting with new positions in the water, I just couldn't hack it. Swimming breaststroke in this outfit was at best, highly challenging and contending the impossible.

Breaststroke was a style I used to be so comfortable with, but now in a wetsuit, it wasn't and it was unsustainable. I went into front crawl from this and with a certain degree of joy found with a degree of comfort. More buoyancy for breathing on the side was a significant advantage. It was comfortable making the front crawl strokes glide with ease through the waters much quicker than anything experienced before. Right at this point, I saw why it was such a substantial advantage and favoured by swimmers that were speed merchants.

When lying on my back, there was no need for waving hands or kicking legs for my head to remain above the waterline. I could have fallen asleep and been relatively safe with no danger of sinking even with air expelled from my lungs. It was like lying on an airbed!

The tables had turned. I felt much more at ease with front crawl than breaststroke in saltwaters and this now leads to a dilemma. If I do the 2-mile event in London with a wetsuit, I won't be able to make any progress or sustained swimming with breaststroke. Breaststroke was my lifeline in terms of endurance and recovery and a relief from the front crawl. What do I do now?

The wetsuit experience, therefore, was a 'bitter-sweet' one. If the London waters are below a specific temperature, the wetsuit will become compulsory, which meant that there would be no choice other than using front crawl. As the wetsuit swim experience told me, I'd be exhausted by the energy needed to get my head above water for breath in breaststroke and wasn't a viable swimming option right now.

My preference in the light of things would be to swim without a wetsuit as in the school pool using a mix of breaststroke and front crawl. There would be a tow float there for panics and breaks when they happen. Either way, I have to focus on the front crawl now if water temperatures dictate wetsuit wearing.

It only took one minute to take off the wetsuit and a well-earned refreshing non-alcoholic beer sunk in the stifling heat which had now gone up a few more degrees. On the horizon, waiting was the August 1st. This date was for the final push and working on the front crawl to the best of my ability.

Chapter 7 (August)

Life Line of Training Starts

Training begins again in earnest today as I turned up at the school pool on the first day of August at 09:45. To my dismay, I was refused entry with swarms of children and parents present and told to come back after 16:00. This time I was not put off with the later time given and resigning myself with a day off which was what happened before. I decided to turn up at the suggested time.

Admission paid and into it was into the changing rooms later in the day. Most of the children had finished their swimming sessions and now became a nuisance in the changing rooms – this was no matter as I was focused on going in for a swim, come what may! The shower water was cold as the children had used up all the hot water throughout the day. I moved on to the warm-up stretching exercises before dipping into the pool. Then I had to share a lane with another adult swimmer due to other lanes still being occupied with tail ended children

A repeated two lengths of breaststroke followed by one length of the front crawl was the plan. This sequence was carried out throughout the session over 50 minutes without a break. It was nearly always the case that I couldn't wait for the front crawl to end and get back to the comfort zone of breaststroke. There were occasional fleeting moments; however, where the front crawl nearly bordered on feeling comfortable, but this never lasted long and unsustainable. There was a forced change of lanes three times due to obstructions; those obstructions were children.

This first session went okay, I guess, but there is work to be done; not least on the front crawl. This stroke was a priority with the possibility of wetsuits being compulsory in the event next month.

Yet again, I have to put my hand up and say that I do not particularly enjoy the swimming. It is just the challenge of beating my phobia of water in front of me that keeps me going not the actual sport. With this, I'm not looking forward to the next session knowing that I have to push myself in an area I am uncomfortable with, in this case, the front crawl. What keeps me motivated now was the fact that there are less than six weeks to the event. After this, I can knock swimming on the head once that medal dangles around my neck.

There is an opportunity to go swimming tomorrow, but it will have to wait until the following Monday - always a good day to start things up. The plan is for a three-session week for next week and then see how I feel after that.

Light at the End of the Tunnel?

Today I turned up at the pool at 16:15 and found that all was calm with just a sprinkling of children playing around. After another 20 minutes and well into the session, the pool was my own, great!

The plan was to build on improving front crawl technique with extended duration. The session, which lasted 50 minutes without a break, was made up repeating the cycle of two lengths breaststroke and two lengths front crawl. As always, it was still relatively stress-free whenever breaststroke came back around to rescue me. There is, however, a hint of getting into a mechanical fashion with the front crawl, albeit never consistent. When there were moments of comfortability, albeit sporadic, it was just trying to find out what caused it.

Fifty minutes later, it was good that I pushed myself with a plan today as it was executed fully and successfully during this session. It felt like I had achieved something and moved on slightly from last week.

It was more than noticeable during the session that I had a little bit of cramp in my calve areas. I worked through this, but a thought came to mind if the waters were colder, the pain would be more difficult to overcome. Muscles seizing up could lead to preventing the completion of the 2-mile event if it was severe enough on the day. I knew dehydration was in place before I started the swim today. The cause must be due to physically intensive chores earlier in the day on the farm in the sweltering heat of over 30C. An increase in liquid intake on future training days was needed to combat this. Also, what didn't help was not consuming any food since my breakfast at 07:00 this morning. Nine hours of fasting isn't ideal for training. This starving process will also have to change.

Nevertheless, the progress seen today was something I was quite content with, especially experiencing the odd glimpse of front crawl moving into the comfort zone.

There is a plan to visit the Black Sea next weekend and again the following weekend. I know a place where there is a stretch of coastline dedicated to scuba divers and swimmers. It is about one kilometre in length, so the plan was to swim that both ways and try and get two kilometres under my belt. It will be with a tow float but no wetsuit though for good reasons.

The first reason is that it is far too hot for a wetsuit with temperatures forecast well over 30C. Secondly, I figured out that swimming in the sea is like swimming in freshwater wearing a wetsuit anyway. With increased buoyancy in saltwater, it was like wearing two wetsuits giving an overly high position that caused my legs to kick air with breaststroke. A bit more of an experienced swimmer kicking in now it seems.

A Bit Tired, But Less Worried

It was nice to get into a routine where I achieved three sessions in seven days. Today the plan was to do reoccurring three lengths of front crawl and two lengths breaststroke. The sessions gave rise to increasing durations of front crawl with ample recovery time in breaststroke.

There were nerves before the session, knowing that three lengths of the front crawl was a challenge and wouldn't be pleasant. I knew there would be a tendency to rush the third length. Pushing hard towards the sanctuary of breaststroke in waiting was the bait. Rushing to the finishing post is historical, so I knew it would reoccur.

The main contention today was to try and avoid that panicky third length and I had the whole session to work on this. Not a chore I was looking forward to, but the critical elements were to try and relax and resist my rushing tendencies. It needed bags of will power and concentration going against the grain of a lifetime of rushing.

Fifty-five minutes achieved today, but it felt like a lifetime. All credit due though as the workout paid dividends. It hadn't gone unnoticed that the front crawl is a speedy stroke, this appeals. The pace almost breaches twice the speed of breaststroke. On odd occasions the freestyle was easy in terms of the effort needed, but only during moments when the correct technique and breathing came together. So with these positive but sporadic elements, I am now less worried about how things are progressing. If only it were more consistent, I would be a happy boy. Well, that's what I have to work on now.

What I also have seemed to have got on top of is the annoying water up to the nose. It used to happen frequently and I used to stop every panic ridden moment. I don't have major panic attacks or stop now, but if water inhaled I just try and blow the water out on the next stroke. This technique adapted and used to solve the issue was a massive chunk of progress in my books. There is still more than a hint of panic when this happens, but I now take the time to think of how to solve the problem before anxiety has a chance to kick in. I recall the times when the reaction was always feet down to the pool floor. It is all down to a matter of rational thinking and having the courage to bear with the uncomfortable moments with self-disciplined tactics. I am quite proud of the fact that all this progress made has been done all on my own without any support other than some like-minded kind folk on RealBuzz.com giving encouragement and suggestions.

More nerves now came into play, knowing that in the next session, I will begin to withdraw the breaststroke recovery periods. And I do lose sleep worrying over this.

Breakthrough!

There was an inherent problem with training that starts after 16:00. Having breakfast at 07:00 each morning, I don't usually eat anything else until the evening 12 hours later when Galia arrived back from work just after 19:00. As mentioned before, nine hours without food is not ideal for long training sessions that start at this time.

Previously, when I started training in spring, the 10:00 start in the pool was ideal with some three hours after a healthy muesli breakfast. The Serpentine event at 09:30 will replicate this sequence of eating three hours before the swim. You couldn't ask for better timing on the day. So what do I do in the meantime to evade hunger pangs and running out of energy late afternoon? Simple, nothing!

Why? Well, I want to lose weight as the wetsuit I have is far too small for me. It would be easier to put on and not strangle me as much if I lost some weight. Besides, I want to get rid of more stomach even though gym work is there on the side. Getting core muscles stronger also reduces potential fatigue on long swims. I am using core muscles to swivel my midriff, which makes it more economical on the energy needed with my arms. So, as you were, no food all day.

The session today was made up of two lengths front crawl and one length breaststroke repeated throughout the course. The idea is to get the front crawl to become a mainstay in swimming style for the first time. To be quite honest, I was quite nervous building up mentally for this over the last few days. It was also a sleepless night and restless day waiting for 16:00 to arrive knowing that there would be more stress now with the comfort zone of breaststroke is gradually withdrawn.

As I pursued the plan, it ended up with a swim for 1 hour 5 minutes non-stop! What was all the fuss about I asked myself? Yes, there were occasions where I wanted the freestyle to end sooner and breaststroke to kick in, but I forced it through. For some reason, the front crawl was now becoming much more relaxed. All the tips I had read up and taken on board seem to have finally paid off. And yes, it is still left only breathing every two strokes in freestyle, but that will do me for now. Relaxing, gliding with delayed strokes and working on body swivels without having to turn my heads to breath all came together on more than a few occasions. It is just a case of getting this to become more consistent. Conceivably I could have gone on longer today, so that was evidence that my swimming fitness was also developing well.

It is now the thought of whether eventually I can get rid of the breaststroke altogether. I never thought that could ever happen - up until now!

There is a view that the event in London for me is a once in a lifetime challenge. That day should be enjoyed and taken in as much as possible. The atmosphere would be great with the event being one of the leading, high-profile open water swims worldwide. The vision I had not so long ago was to just to swim breaststroke with the predicted time of over three hours. With the breathing pattern in breaststroke putting my head up for air every few seconds, I get to see the scenes around me and take in the atmosphere throughout the swim. Taking in the ambience of the occasion was effectively a bonus of taking the course in a high headed slow stroke around the course. Now with the potential of front crawl used like most other swimmers, there will be no opportunity of the head out of the water other than quick glimpses ahead technically called 'sighting'. There was no chance to look around at the antics of other swimmers, crowds watching and cheering you on or opportunities to watch famous London landscapes pass by. The sacrifice of not being able to have sightseeing swimming experience was now in transition to the faster, more efficient front crawl stroke.

For competitive swimmers, using freestyle is used for personal bests and the challenge of beating other competitors. The motive of sightseeing for non-competitive swimmers using breaststroke applies and must appeal to many others. However, I'm sure many, also like me just want to complete the course as that is the challenge whatever stroke is more comfortable.

If the front crawl is the primary stroke, there may well be many moments of breaks using breaststroke or hanging on to the tow float. The pauses give a good reason not just to get my breath back, but to take time and savour the atmosphere, probably opportunities to communicate with other gangs of struggling swimmers towards the end. I'm sure this will be the case.

Avoiding Monday and the Blues

All weekend, even with distractions at home and on the farm, thoughts of the session today pre-occupied my mind. When Mondays arrive, a monopolised mind full of swimming anticipations made it near impossible to focus on other things leading up to the 16:00.

There were 101 jobs to be done on the farm with the harvesting, processing and preserving fruit and vegetables that has now begun in earnest. These chores take the best part of the day and would typically involve going beyond the 16:00 deadline set for the pool. It transpires that I don't commit myself to any of the chores on the farm on Mondays to avoid the possibility and temptation of missing the swim. Most of my day now was pottering around the home playing around in the kitchen, making homemade food and drinks from farm produce harvested. There was also jarring, bottling up and subsequent labelling chores in await. Conceivably these chores could be done away from the farm and in the main was. I knew that a venture to the farm that would undoubtedly tempt me away and swimming fall of the end.

If there is one thing that I want to get away from, it is the lifetime habit of being rushed with everything that comes my way. I left the traits of leading a rushed rat race life in the UK in 2017. However, try as I might not allowing that to infiltrate into my lifestyle here, it is always a constant uphill battle. It is not made easier by setting too many unnecessary goals all the time that only a Brit would make, unlike Bulgarians, who wouldn't dream of making goals just for the sake of it. The 2-mile swim event is an excellent example of this. The only person here in Bulgaria interested in doing this was me, despite trying to get others to join in on the act. Everyone here thinks my application and pursuit of this swim was a pointless exercise. They find it strange that with all the chores that I have at the moment during the growing season on the farm, I subject myself to more work and stress with this swimming challenge. They think I'm crazy riding my bike for no apparent reason other than the love of cycling, the joy, fitness and multiple health benefits associated with it. Many here in Bulgaria for some reason, just don't get it or understand a culture I can't get rid of!

At 61 years of age now, people around me just can't understand why I can't just 'let things go' and 'enjoy life' without trying to test myself all the time. It must be that the concept of 'enjoy' is only understood with a different perspective. Doing nothing is not enjoyable but frustrating from my view, although to others, it may well be enjoyable. How can you do nothing anyway? It is impossible. Even when you are dead, you are in the process of doing something; decomposing! It is only until that process is completed you finally arrive at the point of not doing anything and only because you are not there anymore.

I now have the nickname of 'Tiger,' from a few here. I guess that's a compliment. They see a man at a loose end who fills all his spare time with cycling, running and now swimming just for the hell of it, then added to these by running a farm full-time. They just don't see the logic of all the physical work on the farm supplemented with more physical work. My answer to that is all the food and drink tastes much better after a hard day of physical work. And it does!

After a good swimming session last Friday, I wanted to build on that, but I had doubts whether that I could achieve that today. Why?

Every time I go to the pool on a Monday with a plan, that plan never seems to be able to be carried through. The history of failures is because Monday is probably the busiest day of the week in the pool and with that no free-swimming lanes. I had a gut feeling that the same would happen today.

It's 16:10 and I'm at the pool. The first thing I noticed was an echoing din coming from the pool area; I hear this entering the reception. The noise spelt out the fact that the pool was indeed full of swimmers. As I went through the process getting changed, showered and finally entered the pool area, my assumption was correct. There were absolutely no free lanes with each lane having at least three occupants. There was the far side lane with the two water filters sticking out on the side had the fewest users. That was the glaringly obvious lane choice for me at this point

The plan was to have three of front crawl and one length breaststroke to build up front crawl duration with reduced recovery time with the breaststroke. This plan was a complete waste of time, given the situation I was in sharing this lane.

There were two gipsies amongst others using this lane and they didn't have any respect for others in their wake. They hit me on countless occasions with knocks to the head, midriff and legs. There was no effort to accommodate me with space when passing on their part. I made all the effort to avoid battering to no avail. There wasn't one length where I had a clear swim of front crawl. I had to revert to a slim-line doggy style breaststroke each time these guys approached. There were no other options other than to shy away from them for at least 30 minutes. There was a stop, start and wait for them to pass tactic with no chance for working on the front crawl technique or any other type of continuous swim. I was frustrated and down with this situation. I knew that this might well be the same at the Serpentine event with more aggressive and greedy swimmers, albeit they will be going the same way as me. Each pass made with another swimmer felt like a confrontation. It was a throwback to past panic situations each time hits landed with gasps for air, then my feet immediately falling to the floor each time.

I changed lanes eventually to join three other swimmers and the same situation arose. The big issue was front crawl swimming means you can't see where you are going without raising your head to 'sight' ahead. In a pool with a length of 17 metres and three other swimmers, it meant that sightings were needed every few metres. With the head-up often, the whole concept of gliding through the water with a streamlined body goes to pot and the legs consequently dip as a result. Also, the rushed breathing panicked with the looking up, the whole scene is uncoordinated and it ends up in complete chaos.

I gave up front crawl and carried on with breaststroke resigned to not being able to train under these circumstances. Being frustration, I finally left the pool only after a 45-minute session being a pointless exercise in my view.

Monday yet again brings about a plan that failed. Maybe next week I will start on Tuesday which might work, besides there is a sea swim planned for Sunday.

Getting back home, I was quite depressed. After all the waiting over the weekend and putting chores and other commitments off for today's session, it turned out to be a complete failure. With five weeks to go, there is always going to be a stumble or two. Added to the insult was finding out that I now had a verruca on my left big toe. This infection must be from the pool or changing room area from one or more of the kids. I always wear my rubber-based sandals in the changing rooms, shower and walking up to the pool entrance area. Even with these precautions taken, it wasn't a mystery this annoying virus is now with me. Another issue to contend with in swimming pools, I guess.

I will get back to the pool on Wednesday for another session and see how that fairs.

A Game of Two Unequal Halves

After Monday's session, it was doom and gloom in terms of expectations getting opportunities to work on the front crawl technique and endurance. Still, I continued to pursue making my way to the pool again in the sweltering heat touching 34C today.

There were about the same amount of young folk in the pool today as the previous session as I took time deliberating which lane to choose. The choice had to be the lane most likely to give me the least grief. There was a centre lane with crowds of kids playing around about at both ends, but only one boy swimming. The swimmer was busting a gut for two lengths and then taking a breather. That moment was the cue to get some front crawl in each subsequent time there was a pause for his recovery.

As things stood, my daily progressive plans had utterly gone to pot. The Monday session planned was a 3:1 ratio of front crawl and breaststroke and today was to build this up to 4:1. There was no chance of getting this far as things had turned out recently.

Once again, it was impossible to have any continuous swimming with other swimmers heading towards me in the lane. It is a matter of not being able to swim forward blind with freestyle as the thought of a collision happening was high risk. Even with just one other person in the lane with the length only 17 metres long, it is only a matter of some 30 seconds each time a passing occurs.

Breaststroke was reverted to for 45 minutes with some sporadic front crawl done with anxiety not knowing what of when hazards were coming towards me. Being reluctantly resigned to work just on breaststroke I wasn't extending myself aerobically, but what else could I have done in this situation? Better than nothing though.

Eventually, the child left the waters and I had 15 minutes alone in the lane. It felt like a great weight lifted off my shoulders. I started again with front crawl and the 3:1 ratio missed on Monday's session. It ended up with around 20 lengths being achieved non-stop in this drill, other than stopping to turn each length of course. I was slightly out of breath throughout this repetition but amazed myself with the result. I didn't feel entirely comfortable in terms of relaxing as much as I would have liked. This uneasiness I'm sure was to do with the mental hangover anxiety caused by the fear of collisions experienced in the previous 45 minutes.

All this swimming in traffic I reflected was good for the actual event where there won't be just one swimmer but hundreds. There is a grace in the fact that all swimmers in the Serpentine will be going in the same direction. Also, my snail pace means that I won't be bumping or hitting into swimmer's feet ahead of me, just attacks from behind

Today then was a game of two unequal halves. With one hour total in the water the first 45 minutes of sheer hell and frustration with the second period of 15 minutes, distanced well away from a 'hellish' environment and productive.

Friday beckons and I think it may be a good idea to arrive 30 minutes later than I have been in recent times. It seemed like there would be a good chance of the kids finishing and a lane left for myself with this ploy.

The thought of the event only five weeks away made me feel nervous. Throughout the last six months, training has been erratic, but I do think that others are more than likely to be in the same boat as me on the day, (forgive the pun). Perhaps we could paddle along together for company and encourage each other, especially over the last half mile, this may well be needed.

Back at home speaking to Galia, I was telling her that after five weeks she won't see me in that swimming pool again because I don't enjoy it. She thought I would have given up by now with the issues and can't understand why I continue to do something I don't like. This explanation was something I couldn't convey as the reasoning and justifications just don't fit well into Bulgarian culture.

It will be back on land with my bicycle conquering local mountains again soon. The Surrey 100-mile ride again next year…? Whoooo! There I go again, setting up other challenges. Why do I do that?

Forced Swim

The idea today was to get into the pool slightly later than previous days to avoid the backend of the children that had not finished their swimming sessions. From what I have seen, the pool is usually clear of kids leaving only a couple of adults swimming by 16:45.

It was a struggle to get motivated to go swimming today. I had to force myself to get out of the door and make tracks to the pool. The following planned training programme felt like chores I wouldn't enjoy in the least. The swim preoccupied my mind all day. The only reason I went, in the end, was the thought of feeling angry with myself if I didn't go. It felt like a countdown to putting my finger into a flame very mindful that the mental anticipation is as almost as painful as being burnt.

With the preoccupation of thoughts of the swim all day, just like before, the whole day is affected. The trip to the farm cancelled and I spent most of the day in the kitchen making tomato chutney and roasting peppers harvested recently. It almost feels like being in prison or a slave to the session ahead. Despite being on task, this torturous mental countdown was ticking away with reoccurring thoughts of not wanting to go and suffer in that big pool of suffocating water.

Today for a change, my core muscle gym session was done before I went to the pool not afterwards as usual. The reason being there wouldn't be enough time after the swim as I have to prepare dinner for us to eat at 19:00. Perhaps I might add two gym sessions, one before and another after the swim from next week. I enjoy the pain of the workouts and I think that to build up more strength in the core muscles wouldn't be a bad thing. If there were a pain barometer, the fitness session would register far higher than any swimming session. The enjoyment and reward I get out of 'healthy physical pain' must be due to the absence of water and the fear of suffocation. Unfortunately, swimming is difficult without water!

It was getting on with things now as the front door closed behind me. As I made my way down two flights of stairs and into the open-air heading towards the school complex, it felt like the hardest part of the day was done, namely getting that first foot out of the front door.

I arrived at the school at around 16:30. In the pool, there was a sprinkling of children, but fortunately, this did not affect me as I opted to share a lane with another adult.

For some reason, my goggles were continually filling up with water. After each length, I had to stop, empty the water and tighten the goggles. The numerous adjustments didn't make any difference to the leaking over the first half dozen lengths. Having to stop each time and repeat the process was annoying and naturally disrupted the swim. Eventually, the problem was solved, but it remains a mystery as to why it took so long to get these goggles watertight. This leakage hadn't happened for ages, why now?

Back to uninterrupted swimming without goggle issues, I was still trying to avoid colliding with my lane sharer. The front crawl stroke style needed to be changed to breaststroke on each approach to get by. There were a few occasions where a length of the front crawl was possible without the interference of having to pass the swimmer but sporadic, which was frustrating.

During this time, it was difficult to relax while swimming having to shorten my strokes with breaststroke to reduce the widths needed to the swimmer in my lane. Avoid swimmers in the next lane being close to the dividing ropes meant once again shortened strokes. My natural stroke was not possible for the most. There was no time where an opportunity for regular swimming pattern to take place with dodging people all the time. There was no comfort zone throughout and it incurred stress. This sharing of a lane I might add was with a considerate swimmer.

Eventually, as time ticked on, I got a lane to myself, the nearside lane with the two water filters - that did me nicely. It was straight into the front crawl and I covered a total of 30 lengths non-stop which equated to over half a kilometre! I stopped there happy with that achievement albeit only comfortable with the front crawl style for few of those lengths.

I had only been in the water 45 minutes today, but it could have been very different, I may well have not turned up at all.

One of the main reasons I don't feel comfortable in the water now was that my sinuses get filled with fluid. No matter how hard I try to clear my sinuses, they remained blocked, which felt like a form of claustrophobia. After each swim, I found myself trying to empty my sinuses by blocking one nostril and blowing out of the other. This emptying of sinuses usually lasted for at least an hour after each session. There was the unfortunate consequence of leaving a trail of 'snot' in the street all the way home. This disgusting habit was so unlike me on public roads, (and at home, I might add) but I found that it's okay and acceptable to do that here in Bulgaria. Does this happen to all swimmers I thought? If I can avoid my sinuses filling up, I think a little comfort zone will kick in and I can be confident in being able to sustain a front crawl style over more extended periods.

So to try and overcome the sinus issue, I planned to try a nose grip as this could only be the place where the water enters. This nose clamp meant that it would be solely breathing in and out of my mouth. May well be worth a try next outing which will be at sea with a tow float for the first time.

Overall it was a relief more than anything else I turned up to the pool and did the session today. Undoubtedly this is worthy of a big 'pat on the back' for going.

Sea Swimming with Company

It was another trip to the Black Sea early this morning. This time we stayed over just for a one night. I was asked by one of Galia's family to do them a favour by transporting them to the Black Sea as they had reserved an apartment there and no transport. The reward was one night stay free at the holiday apartment and of course, an opportunity to swim came in as part of the bargain.

This opportunity to swim was a big bonus and that was what I did. The idea was to try out the tow float for the first time. It was still in its original wrapping and has been since May. No wetsuit this time, it was far too hot and the saltwater would just balloon me up too far in the water as experienced before.

All set with a buoy as a target which I could see bobbing up and down around 300 to 400 metres out to sea. It was a big grey buoy and the only object on the ocean horizon, so I couldn't miss it or get lost, even without my prescription glasses. In the back of my mind was the fact that for the first time, I was now going to swim in deep waters with no opportunity to put feet down if a panic situation occurs. I did wonder whether this attempt would have happened if I wasn't using the tow float.

Amidst playful holidaymakers in the holiday mood, I made my way out to sea. It wasn't long before I was beyond the earshot of maddening crowds. It was quite surreal to suddenly have no noise other than my own created from a little splashing from stroke cycles and breathing.

Starting with breaststroke just to get warmed up, it was no time before had the urge to transgress into front crawl. It was nice and relaxed feeling comfortable with left side breathing and proper technique coming into play. The thought of moving faster using less energy as opposed to the laboured dragging breaststroke appealed greatly at this stage. I could now do this as training in the pool has paid off.

Every five or six strokes, I looked up to sight where the buoy was. I was veering to the right, so I adjusted my position accordingly each time this happened. With my breathing solely my left and a more vigorous left-sided stroke, a little veering to one side was not unexpected.

All was going great as I passed by the point of the rock jetties either side of me and into distinctly cooler waters. The sea bed was now completely out of sight through my goggles looking down. It was a type of vertigo that came over me, but I bravely pushed forward carrying on out to sea. The tow float hit my feet every so often, especially when in breaststroke mode. However, this was not a hindrance but more of a relief as it reminded me that my Guardian Angel was there still attached to me.

Then all of a sudden, a great fear came over me as I peered into the water. I sighted swarms of jellyfish around me in all directions. Each time saw a jellyfish ahead, my arm adjusted to try and avoid hitting it. These creatures start to invade these waters in mid-summer and the sea becomes inundated with them by late summer. I somehow didn't account for this hazard. They do administer a nasty sting if touched or provoked and I was now in the midst of thousands of them.

I was now almost at the point of reaching the big grey buoy but decided to avert due to the jellyfish invasion. My relaxed and consistent stroke technique was currently being severely affected by trying to avoid striking jellyfish. It wasn't pleasant swimming with these silent stingers as I made my way back to the beach. It was such a relief reaching the holidaymakers still splashing around in waters in an area now completely void of jellyfish. Not quite sure why are not found nearer the beach, perhaps they prefer the cooler waters further out.

I swam with a tow float in deep waters, both first for me and with this, I was quite content. Jellyfish aside, I would have reached that outer buoy with ease and probably done a few more rounds there and back. That's confidence for you.

It was only a 10-15 minutes swim, but the tow float made a big difference giving confidence in deep waters. The front crawl felt as comfortable as it has ever been. I'm sure this was because of the saltwater raising my body, making the breathing more comfortable. The wetsuit should have the same raising effect in freshwater.

There is no swimming planned in the school pool back in Yambol on Monday, but there will be on the following day. A Tuesday swim this week to avoid the Monday crowds which seem to hit each time on that first day of the week.

Jellyfish - My Swimming Companions Today

On reflection, this was a big day purely from the fact that I was swimming in deep waters and although there was a scariness about it I coped with that well. The tow float was the key to this as I know the fear of deep waters would be something that would have given me significant anxiety and panic without it to the extent of not swimming.

Plans now are to work with front crawl trying to get in as many lengths as possible without breaks.

A Real Training Session

Is it Tuesday already? Yes! Then it is a trip to the local school swimming pool as planned.

Again, I wasn't that keen to go knowing that it would be an hour of doing something I had to do rather than wanting to do. The motivation is purely down to the fear of not preparing enough for the London event, which now is just over four weeks away.

Trying to turn up later to the pool to avoid kids is difficult as it is against my nature. Today I arrived at the pool at precisely 16:26 although I intended to get there at 16:45. After a lifetime of turning up early for work each day, this remains a habit that I consistently fail to break.

I knew that the earlier arrival meant having to share a lane with kids for the around 15 minutes. If I had turned up at the planned time, I would have had a lane to myself for the whole one hour. It makes complete sense turning up later, but so hard for me to do!

For the first 15 minutes, swimming with breaststroke was the forced-choice due to children traffic. This situation was my fault for an earlier start than planned. It was so comfortable with the breaststroke, but as always, the slowness was a big frustration. I knew that this style of swimming could go on for hours without fatigue, but then going nowhere requires the same amount of energy.

Into the front crawl, at last, trying to focus on maintaining proper technique, relaxing and gliding as much as possible. However, it wasn't comfortable and indeed more difficult than it was in the sea two days ago. I was lying lower in the water and felt like I needed more effort to stay up and swim without that extra buoyancy. The wetsuit would surely correct that issue in the 2-mile London event.

No trouble with water in the goggles today and there was a reason for that. They were strapped on from the outset as tight as I could bear. After 20 minutes, it felt like I had been punching in the face with the continuous pressure applied. Unfortunately, there is no room for compromise here. Unless they are as tight as a duck's arse, water seeps in. I'm sure the goggles aren't suited to my face but haven't disposable income to just splash out on another decent pair. I will just have to put up with some discomfort, besides which there is only one month to go and an end to this painful saga. I have felt like this about the 2-mile challenge and have done for quite a while now. Get the business done, claim the medals and return to a life on land without stress couldn't come too soon.

Up and down, up and down continuously in front crawl. It does take a while to get into some kind of rhythm, not as easy as it needed complete focus throughout. I have to admit there were a few rare moments where I felt comfortable with the stroke during this session. I ploughed on with the thought that one day, leading up to the event, perhaps I might get that feeling that this stroke may become second nature.

As time went on, my sinuses were gradually filling up with water again. Water seems to trickle in bit by bit compounding the uncomfortable feeling. I did try a nose clamp on Sunday, but it ended up with my nose scored by the unforgiving hard plastic clips. My nose ended up bleeding and I gave up with it feeling quite sore since leaving a scar as a reminder. The wrong choice of Chinese made nose clamps I guess, but I didn't have any other versions.

It was a full dedicated 40 minutes non-stop front crawl before I warmed down with two lengths of breaststroke to finish.

There was a certain degree of aerobic effort needed during that 40 minutes turning the session into a proper workout. This workout was unlike breaststroke, where it didn't feel like I had ever taxed myself aerobically; apart from those first couples of attempts when starting in spring. If I can get the freestyle effort down to a minimum, there is an air of confidence that I could go the whole 2-mile duration in front crawl with a wetsuit.

It turned out to be a good workout today and I will try to extend that time of 40 minutes on the next outing. A more significant quest is trying to turn up for the sessions at a later time. With a lane to myself from the outset, there is a whole hour waiting for me. Being forced to use breaststroke while sharing a lane with habitual earlier arrivals is just pointless.

A Few Things Understood

It was 36C plus in Yambol today and I had been working on the farm in that temperature until midday. After returning home, I just conked out on my bed for two hours, probably due to heat exhaustion.

Earlier that morning, my right shoulder was giving me pain, which had been the case for a few days now.

The cause could be fighting against the power of a petrol-driven rotavator on the land or possibly carrying Galia's grandchild on my shoulders at the weekend. Regardless of possible causes, painkillers in my system this morning and once again after my two-hour recovery in bed.

I don't usually take painkillers unless pain is unbearable, in this instance it was.

With medication administered, it was all systems go and to the pool with the shoulder pain subsided somewhat much to my relief. The last thing I needed was another barrier preventing training sessions with only four weeks until the event. There was another play on my will power to get me to the pool again today. With the thought of the swimming quest ending soon, this certainly helped motivate me to turn up for training this time around.

I was in the pool at 16:50; this was the latest I had turned up to date. Even so, there were still children playing around when lane hunting. I noticed one adult swimmer beckoning me to share his lane. He told me it much was better sharing with him than the kids and I didn't need much persuasion and took up his offer.

Even though there was just one other person in the lane, the front crawl, I couldn't practise this consistently. There was an uncontrollable tendency to look up and see where the swimmer was every few seconds. The nervousness took over in this swim, not knowing when he was about to pass; therefore, opportunities to relax and focus on freestyle was impossible. It ended up with a mix of panicky blind front crawl and more observant breaststroke for at least twenty minutes.

If there is one thing I know now, it is a significant stress factor swimming with other swimmers. In the London swimming event, we are all going the same way. That might ease the anxiety a little, but breaststroke is the only answer to alleviating panic with other swimmers. I feel more in control with my head up and a vision of my surroundings.

There is also another thing I have learned today. There is a need to make a minimum of 10 to 15 minutes warming up to get into a relaxed state. The warm-up routine reminds me very much of the systems used with running and cycling. It was always uncomfortable for the first 15 minutes or so until you got your second wind when the comfort zone kicks in being aerobically stable. Then you just get gradually more tired as you go on.

With this as insight, it is now my plan to start the event with breaststroke for two reasons. Firstly, there will be hundreds of other swimmers crowding out at the start and the last thing anyone needs is panic from the outset. Once swimmers have strung out, front crawl can then kick in. Secondly, this will allow me to warm up and get into my second wind ready for the bouts of front crawl. This plan made complete sense to me given where I was at this stage both technically and mentally.

My shared lane became my lane after some 20 minutes and continuous front crawl began in earnest. What a big difference it made to the focus on the swimming style having the lane to myself with no distractions or hazards. It wasn't entirely comfortable though, as I found myself racing with others in adjacent lanes. The aerobic practice was beneficial, so I wasn't that bothered to let my natural competitiveness tendencies dictate on odd moments.

It ended up with at least 35 minutes front crawl non-stop and was more than content with that achievement.

There was an issue with some of the kit as I decided to try different earplugs today. The coned silicon plugs always had given me pain after the insertion at around the 30-minute mark. A new pair tested were a soft silicone material that had to be forced into the ear subsequently moulding itself into the shape of the inner ear. That was fine for a while then they began to seep in water after only 20 minutes. I ended up with water in my ears by the end of the session, a big irritant for me. I'd instead put up with short term pain than ears full of water which teases and annoys for days on end. The uncomfortable issues with swimming seem never-ending.

Somehow my goggles didn't seep water today even though the straps weren't on that tight. These goggles are so temperamental presenting an enigma as to why they work one day and not another.

There was no hot water in the shower after the swim for the second time this week. The cold was only a problem for a few seconds once acclimatised. Besides, it was 32C when I stepped outside into the blinding sun. A 10-minute walk back home was made stopping for a vending machine coffee bought en route.

The thought of only having to go to the pool a handful of times now is quite calming. These training sessions had become a major chore, especially in recent times. I would rather be doing other things in this glorious weather than forcing myself to go to the pool. Every morning I apologise to my road bike for ignoring it and give the tyre a little pat. On my return back from the UK on the 22nd September after the swimming event, I will be back on the bike and hitting the roads again, breathing in fresh air without thought or timing involved. I have also registered and applied for next year's Surrey 100 bike ride. However, I know logistically and financially it won't be possible. Dream on!

A trip to the Black Sea was planned this coming Sunday with a cunning plan to avoid jellyfish. This plan involved swimming parallel along the coast rather than going directly out to sea. Not too daring, in fact quite cowardly but fulfils a purpose.

One Hour of Discomfort

The planned trip to the Black Sea for a swimming workout in the sea just didn't happen last Sunday. This disappointment was for reasons I don't want to go into detail. The trip was cancelled at the last moment and left me frustrated and angry. I will say that it was an occasion where other people let you down, but you just carry on regardless of the betray of trust.

On a different note, a previous problem that had raised its ugly head is solved. The verruca that appeared on my big left toe a while ago is history. It took a while for the planned 'do it yourself' surgery to take place but was administered successfully. I just couldn't face going through the masses of expensive 'over the counter' treatments from chemist shops, so I decided to solve the problem myself. The process involved a certain degree of self-mutilation using a combination of a razor blade, a pin and tweezers.

Initially, I shaved the area with the razor until blood ran from the epicentre of the verruca, then covered it with a plaster. I went through well over ten plasters during the next 48 hours with the continuous stream of blood. Plasters don't last long in the heat here and working in sandals on the land just shorten their durability to stay on even further. Every other day the shaving process was repeated until new blood was flowing again. It was a painful process, but the first part of the plan was well on the way to eradicating the problem.

After four days, traces of the dark demon verruca were almost completely gone. After the continuous razored assaults, using a pin, I pricked the area to loosen the tender skin surrounding the verruca. Then, using a pair tweezers to pick out of the debris left behind. Amongst the dead skin debris, the constantly disturbed verruca roots lay dead and defeated having given up the fight. Hey presto, problem solved! In less than a week the verruca has vanished albeit having to put up with another week of ever-decreasing pain after the butchering. I just didn't have the patience to wait for conventional treatment which could take weeks or months to work if at all. In the future will have to be more careful treading in the school swimming pool complex.

It was back to swimming matters. With no swim Sunday, it would be tempting to use the school pool on Monday. Tuesday, however, was the better option with an afterthought because of the history of issues with Monday swims.

With daily workout routines working on my core muscles, it wasn't too much of a discern missing one session anyway. The habits of planking are something I will continue after the swimming subsides. Since I had started planking, there have had no niggling pains in my legs or lower back, which had plagued me for years and this reason alone gives reason to continue. There is nothing negative about doing the workouts and all you need is a floor!

At present, the plank routines have developed well with each session now lasting 16 minutes. These sessions take place after I returned home from a swimming session or late afternoon if no swim. These are performed six days a week with a rest day on Sunday. The planking sequence is done all without pauses in the following timed sequence:

- **5 mins. basic plank**

- **1 min. right side plank**

- **1 min. basic plank**

- **1 min. left side plank**

- **1 min. basic plank**

- **2 mins. plank with alternate 10 secs. left/right leg raised**

- **5 mins. basic plank to finish**

This plank routine totals 16 minutes.

At the end of each session, a constant stream of sweat drips onto the floor from the effort. With this, there could have almost been another swimming session as I collapse into that gathered pool of sweat! It is very uncomfortable with a tremendous amount of fatigue getting through these planking sessions. It involves some degree of psychology going through the torture it holds. The main tactic is trying to focus and place the mind on something obscure, so you are mentally away from the reality of pain. The benefits and rewards of these sessions are both physically and mentally satisfying. It was strange that unbearable pain from planking sessions was something I enjoyed, but not the discomfort of mental pain and panic from swimming.

It was a 17:45 start when I entered the pool area today and only two other swimmers in the water. It felt good knowing that in hindsight, turning up Tuesday was the right decision.

All dry area warm-up stretching routines had been done and then straight into the water. I made a point of ensuring my goggles didn't leak while bobbing to avoid having to stop and adjust them later. The intention was to start by doing around ten lengths of breaststroke as a warm-up. The extended limbering up was in the knowledge of the need to get into a second wind before starting the front crawl. Well, that's what I thought initially. Then, after four lengths of breaststroke, I got bored and impatient and went directly into front crawl some six lengths earlier than scheduled. Did the lack of warm-up make any difference to the front crawl drill?

One hour later, it was a proud man leaving the pool. I knew at this point that I could manage over a mile in the freestyle having swum nearly two kilometres in this session without a break.

Throughout the swim, I have to say that it wasn't comfortable. There was an undulating range of physical and mental phases I went through during this session. It was always a relief to grab my breath in every two strokes on the left. I want to stop many times, but my mind was still motivating me thinking I only have to do this for a few more weeks, so I ploughed on. I recall one point where near the end of the swim where there was a glimmer of comfort. When this happened, I put more effort into the strokes speeding up with loads of energy to spare. This new ability to push the swim surprised me, but a greater surprise was being able to slow down again after the sprint in front crawl style to recover...! That was amazing knowing I now had this in my tank.

There is something that sticks in my head with pool swimming. Every length, there is a break to turn. Even though I try to keep the breathing rhythm at the same tempo, there is that inevitable stop, pause and start up again. I don't push off when starting up again as mentioned before I feel that is cheating. I'm sure it won't make much difference with a single two-mile length to complete, but these little regular 17 metre breaks are always niggling away in the back of my mind. Also, no swimmer traffic today, but if there were it would take up more energy with the anxiety and stress that appears alongside. I can probably give as good as I get when it comes to jostling, fighting and sticking up for myself for space out of the water, but in the water I am vulnerable!

With just over three weeks to the event, my only worries that came to mind were needing the toilet if I'm wearing a wetsuit. I don't think I could bring myself to wet myself, although this was quite common from what I read. As for number twos, well I guess you would have to leave the water for that. It was a nightmare thinking of that eventuality which has to be the worst-case scenario for any swimmer in a wetsuit.

In the past, I have had issues with being trapped in places and wanting the toilet. Trains, cars, lifts or any situation where there was a hold up for extended periods without toilet facilities is a big problem for me. There is also a big fear of going to new places without prior knowledge of toilet locations. These toiletry issues followed me into sports and especially marathon running and long cycling events. They were many times caught out needing to go while competing. Sometimes I just got away with it, but other times I hadn't. The open countryside is salvation for wanting the toilet with the preference always to cycle or jog outside urban areas. The rural area, of course, gives me relief both mentally with knowledge of natural toilet hideaways such as trees and bushes around.

Wearing a wetsuit to me feels like an urban trap and once again, the return of the fear of being caught out wrapped up. Following a strict dietary regime to avoid such instances wherever possible has always been in place. However, sometimes just a change of location upsets the stomach regardless of careful nutritional precautions. I will be 3000 kilometres away from home at the London event and that change of location will inevitably play games with my stomach and that is a big worry. I had been advised by others to pack some Imodium or something similar in my minimal luggage for that weekend as insurance. Having never done that medication trick before, looking at the side effects, it feels like it would be falling into an area of other unknown risks.

Toilet talk aside, Thursday beckons with the next planned swimming session with nothing after that until the following Tuesday. There are no safe open waters to try out freshwater swimming in my wetsuit. Worn only once in open waters, and that was in seawater, is a concern. Seemingly it will now only be worn next at the London event without any further testing before this. I will just have to try it on dry a few times if the weather cools down a bit here. There has been nothing less than 30C temperatures for as long as I can remember here in recent times with no abate according to local weather experts.

Training on a Fruitful Day

For the first time, there wasn't that gnawing anticipation and tension that continually preoccupied my mind leading up to going swimming. With all the will power needed to attend previous sessions, there was no need to force me to go today. I wasn't that keen, but less than usual and I put this down solely to curiosity. In the last session, I managed one hour of continuous front crawl. The interest was whether I could repeat this today. Guess that anomaly was the challenge today and I was certainly up for it.

My mind continued to reflect on last Tuesday's session. I knew I had to push myself hard to keep going on that front crawl and for the main, it was still uncomfortable. I always had to force myself to duck my head under the water after every other stroke laboured me mentally. There was still that slight fear of not being able to get my head back up clear of water and breathe in each time for some reason. The 'not being able to come up for breath' scenario stuck in my mind vividly like a bad dream and was the only reason that I wasn't that keen today. Still, it was better than not having any motivation at all, which was the case up until now. It was a marathon of mental torture, thinking about this and very hard to get it out of my head.

A big part in positive mind games was the final countdown to the event. With planned training sessions now down to single figures, this was a big incentive to push me over the last few hurdles.

After looking up a few open water swimming websites, I still am not sure whether a tow float is needed if you wear a wetsuit. Having just worn the wetsuit once in the sea there probably isn't any need. Still, then that was saltwater and the buoyancy the wetsuit gives would be less in freshwater. Come what I may I'll probably use both as double insurance against anxiety and panic that may come about. Stress factors were not only from water issues but from other swimmers. Also, knowing the front crawl is looking as if it is sustainable now, the wetsuit will enhance durability with minimal effort used. My old friend the breaststroke now jilted after eloping with a wetsuit. The decision to ditch breaststroke would have probably been the same without the use of wetsuit given the progress made in the school pool without it.

So back to the present and a short walk to the school pool block. As an experiment, I did my 16 minutes plank routine a quarter of an hour before leaving home rather than after the swim. It doesn't wear me out, so I don't think it makes much difference.

I went through the stretching warm-up processes after a cold shower and all was normal in an almost empty pool and a choice of lanes to use. Just two teenagers were wading about and talking to each other in one lane. Seeing this, it was a wonderful moment with low-stress levels in the pool almost all to myself for an hour. I couldn't ask for anything else!

It was into the water for the planned warm-up with breaststroke. That only lasted two lengths as I went into front crawl. What harm can that do? Well, after three lengths, I was feeling okay and decided to try and breathe on my right side for a dare. Up until now, it has been solely left side breathing, which isn't a significant concern in the pool, but could be in open waters with other people.

Well, what happened? The first stroke took place and it was a quick grab of breath on the right. Suddenly everything seized up and into a big panic moment. I couldn't understand why this was. So another effort was made just for the hell of it and now with anxiety sinking in big time. With the consequences of the experiment, I gave up utterly bamboozled as to why this happens.

Unfortunately, this had a knock-on effect and I hated every moment my head had to sink underwater. Despite efforts to relax and glide, which was what I was doing before experimenting on the right side, it failed. With anxiety present the technique suffered, tension followed and that's how the swim struggled with itself over the next 20 minutes.

The efforts made recapture the breathing technique I had once mastered was now trying. Still, I pushed on in the hope that this would come into play eventually. Another 20 minutes gone and it yet hadn't been resolved. If this happened in the event, what would I do? Well, that is simple; breaststroke would come into play. Four lengths of lovely comfortable breaststroke were like revisiting a long lost friend. After working so hard on the front crawl in discomfort, I'd almost forgot how mentally calm this breaststroke was. Quite clearly, it was useful to use as a therapy for relaxing again.

It wasn't long before getting back into a front crawl, but still, it was a big struggle. On my previous session, the gliding was working needing ten-cycle stroke from one end of the pool to the other. In this session, I took 12, so it was pretty obvious something was wrong. Perhaps not enough warm-up time with breaststroke to start? Trying out the right-side breathing and getting into a panic from that and not recovering? Workout with the plank session before the swim instead of after? No other people were swimming to distract, impede or subconsciously compete with, so it couldn't be that. Or was it the fact that I was dehydrated from work in the farm earlier? I didn't have my regular isotonic non-alcoholic beer lunchtime after grafting in the intense heat all morning.

It was just over 40 minutes of front crawl and 15 of breaststroke today in a virtually empty pool. Not even an hour of swimming had passed and I was now feeling quite sleepy. I wanted to close my eyes and swim blind towards the end of the session. Tiredness, illness or just a one-off day for swimming? It was a shame as the pool conditions and the environment was perfect to put in a good training session today.

As the swim came to a close, my thoughts turned to if I felt like this on event day, what would I do? The answer I gave myself was quite simple, carry on regardless with breaks if needed. That positive self-answering didn't make me feel too bad about today.

As I arrived home, a belly ache kicked in and it was a trip to the toilet with an upset stomach. What caused this? Well, it was a quite simple answer to work out. On the farm, while harvesting, I was eating part of the harvest including, apples, pears, figs, sweetcorn and grapes. This extra food was on top of my regular healthy diet today. Because I ate loads of fresh home-grown mouth-watering fruit, this was the reason I wasn't quenching for the regular non-alcoholic beer after work. It was quite apparent the stomach issues came from this and probably why the swim was a struggle. It won't happen next time with this swooping learning curve.

Fruit Fresh From the Farm

Away we go for a sea swimming session on Sunday if all goes to plan - famous last words. We'll see. We do not have to rely on others this time, so it should be okay!

Chapter 8 (September)

Life on an Ocean Wave

Friday was a bad day. I scolded my right hand with an exploding pressure cooker and it had been giving me grief, constant pain and subsequently blisters from the burns. Galia wouldn't allow me to use that pressure cooker again as this was the second time this has happened. I think she's concerned not just about my health, but the possibility of not having an apartment to come home to one day. Things don't stop though, you just have to try and carry on the best you can. The farm has no empathy for my wounds, the fruit and vegetable growth won't pause and now it is only three weeks to the swimming event. These times are crucial for pushing me further with swimming endurance.

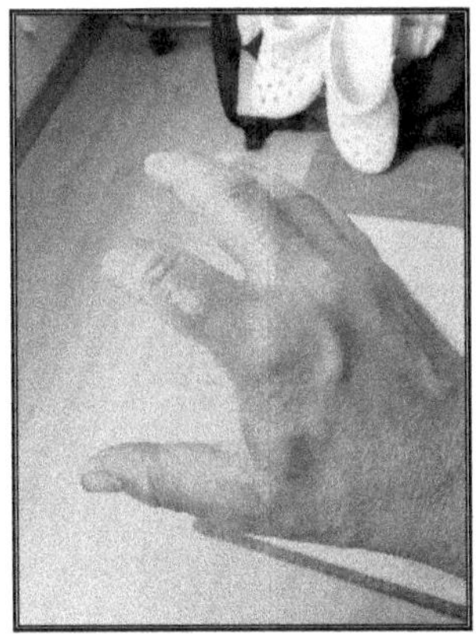

Painful Scolded Hand

As planned, we travelled to the Black Sea late Saturday afternoon to stay in a coastal town called Ravda. The accommodation was a filthy pit hole, but it was cheap. It worked out at around 50 leva for two nights so we shouldn't grumble, but we did. The grumble was in the form of an honest review on the Booking.com site. Subsequently, we got justifiable financial compensation for our efforts!

Out of the accommodation pit with our beach outfits on, we walked the 150 metres to the beach with a warm sunny, but blustery outlook. While Galia lounged on the beach, I planned to go for a short swim just to get the feel of open waters again, with a longer swim sketched in for tomorrow morning. Looking at the waves you could see the surf was up. I also noticed that no one had umbrellas up, understandably as they wouldn't last long with the wild gusts of wind which picked up sand and blew it in your face. A bit dodgy for swimming, especially without a tow float that wasn't with me as it was only going to be used in the longer swim the next day.

So I bottled it. It was now just looking at buoys in the sea and planning the route for tomorrow's session. It was a nervy moment thinking if the windy conditions where the same the following day it could be quite dangerous. Added to this, I couldn't see anyone else in the waters in these conditions. My thoughts suddenly got distracted and distanced from weather conditions and focused on the possible issues of jellyfish again.

With the apartment we were staying at being such a disgrace, not least with beds smelling of stale sweat, we decided to have an evening out away from the stench. The idea was to have a few drinks to help us get through the night. This provision didn't work for a good night with us not getting much sleep at all. To compound things further, we both had a little hangover the following morning. Nevertheless, after downing a Bulgarian pastry and a yoghurt drink for breakfast, we were early birds off to the beach at around 09:30. Unfortunately, we didn't find any decent free spaces to settle and had to hunt for around half an hour for a patch. This was due to the flocks of earlier early birds.

The wind was up again, but not as severe as yesterday. My hat was still on at this point, so that was a good sign. With earplugs in and tow float attached, I said goodbye to a relaxed but curious Galia who was probably glad of an opportunity to catch up on some beach sleep.

Many rocks were barring my bare-footed entry into the sea, with the danger of cuts and lacerations high on the risk list. This spot we eventually found was free for a good reason as the entry to the sea for a swim or paddle was hazardous. It was a little walk further along the coast made to find a safer access point and finally a chance to wade in waters and out to sea.

There were regular buoys dotted around 150 metres out. They looked to be at around 200 metres apart spanning the whole bay. I planned to swim out to the nearest buoy and visit each one going north and re-visiting them all going back south travelling parallel to the coast.

To start, I went out to the first buoy with breaststroke and shortly afterwards went into front crawl turning left heading north. All was looking and feeling good at this point. It is so much more comfortable in the sea than the swimming pool. Even though there was a big swell, it didn't affect my stroke too much bar a few bits of untidy splashing arms. With the size of the swell directions were a problem as each time it rose the sighting for the next buoy was obscured. I had to revert to breaststroke, giving me more time between swell rises with eyes above the water to get my bearings. The switch disrupted the constant front crawl swimming, but no big deal because this is the only option open to sight buoys.

There was another issue with sighting, which reminded me of another reason I don't like swimming. Being short-sighted things are blurred without my prescription glasses. In days gone past on rare occasions, I did go in the sea with family or friends and as I recall, these were very lonely experiences. Not being able to recognise people a small distance away without glasses is one of the issues. I also remember getting lost trying to find where we were on the beach on many occasions. The memories came flooding back with difficulties trying to sight those targeted buoys. The fluorescent colour of the buoys help, but there is a degree of confusion sometimes as other floating objects are of a similar colour along the coast and jetties. If I had the money, a pair of prescription goggles this would have solved this issue. All said and done, I coped pretty well without such luxurious aids, besides, the cost would not be a commensurate factor.

As the bottom of the sea disappeared, another sight came into view - Jellyfish! I'd forgotten about them for a while and now got quite frightened seeing them getting so close to me. My reaction and ploy were to shut my eyes when my head is underwater, so I don't see them. On occasions, I feel something on my arm or leg, which I assume is a jellyfish, but I don't see it and carry on. If I get stung, I get stung! This idea was much better than going through the mental stress of seeing the potential sting coming. Despite all this, throughout the swim, somehow I didn't get stung.

I had reached the most northern point buoy without going around a rock reef, then turned around starting back on a southerly route. I must have covered around 400 metres at this point. It was so good to know that both Galia if she isn't asleep and the lifeguards were are all aware of this bright orange tow float skirting behind me along the coast. There were other swimmers out there, but not as far out as I had ventured. I felt quite proud. The 'look at me I'm different from you' is a typical English eccentric feat. With literally thousands of holidaymakers watching as well, it was a most satisfying self-indulgent show.

On the first leg of this circuit, I couldn't see where I was going for most of the time. I don't know how, but while deep in concentration and a 'blind for the most' front crawl, I hit something hard with my right hand. As I naturally stopped treading water, I found that I had just walloped and an older woman. (She looked like she was Russian). I apologised profusely and immediately in Bulgarian. As I looked around, she was the only swimmer I could see for miles (a slight exaggeration). She answered me back, but I had earplugs in and didn't hear what was said. Probably just as well as I might have learnt a few swear words in Russian. What I can't understand is that she must have seen me coming, why the hell she didn't just move to avoid the approaching human torpedo?

Buoys at Regular Intervals

During the swim heading south and all was fine. The seawater had breached into my sinuses, but I put up with that. There was no tiredness, fatigue, or for that matter, stress felt at this point. It is so calm and serene just being on your own in deep seawater away from the maddening crowds.

Was I enjoying myself? Yes, but it was more about showing off. The packed beach was full of onlookers boosting my resolve to continue. It was great for my ego as playing to an audience is something I missed dearly from my past. I used to perform music in bands and orchestras - also, the showman working for many years as a classroom primary school teacher. And then subsequently as a PCV Trainer and theory training classroom teacher with London Buses.

All these vocations also require an element of acting and showmanship. Once a showman always a showman, I guess - I digress.

The southward swim was with the wind behind me. The tow float didn't bother me with a headwind going north. After passing the second buoy on the southern return leg, with the strong tailwind and now out of the harbour shelter, the tow float was hitting my head trying to knock me out. It is only a rubber balloon so not painful, but there was no way I could do front crawl with the float frequently knocking into me. It eventually just got caught up with my arms becoming tangled. No matter how much I tried, the float just wouldn't disobey the wind. I was stuck with no other choice other than to revert to breaststroke once again. It felt a little defeatist having to do this, but circumstances prevail. I wonder what other open water swimmers do when this happens. The result would always end up getting tangled with the chord attaching the tow float to the torso.

This adjustment was the pattern now used as I worked with alternate stroke styles north and south, respectively. I wasn't tired or fatigued throughout the swim, but there was a couple of moments when cramp started to affect my right leg and then my left. With this, I adapted my leg kicks that took up a different position to alleviate that issue. I didn't feel the need to stop and massage at any point, although that was certainly an option up my sleeve if it became too severe. The reason for cramp was apparent, clearly dehydration after a night out in the town with alcohol. Well, after all, we were on holiday for two days!

It was strange putting my feet on the ground when I hit the beach. There were a few tumbles as I gathered the ability to learn to walk again. With my bright tow float to hand, still inflated, I walked proudly back past all the beach folk to where Galia was sunbathing. She hadn't slept and kept an eye on me going up and down the coast sipping one of my non-alcoholic beers. She was quite surprised that I had been out for so long, around 1 hour 20 minutes. The whole time in the sea was swimming non-stop, apart from stopping and apologising to the elderly Russian woman I hit.

I had gone up and down that circuit three or four times, not quite sure of the exact number as I lost count with this adrenalin-filled occasion. The finish found me still feeling strong and quite able to carry on if I had to. The swim was a proud moment knowing that I had done this session. I was 'on a high' which gave licence to enjoy the weekend with this session under my belt.

It remained that once back home in Yambol, the next session was due on the following Tuesday in the familiar school pool. This time without stuffing myself full of farm produce earlier in the day.

The other bonus today was the fact that my severely scolded hand felt soothed in saltwater. The subdued pain had not affected the session with the distraction of excitement during the swim.

An Hour is the Limit

Back home in Yambol and the routine of attending the local school swimming pool is firmly placed back into today's agenda.

After swimming in salt water, there was a tendency to think this session will be harder in freshwater with less buoyancy. With this in mind, my ego surely would be pegged down a bit after the elation of success in sea swimming a couple of days ago. It would be back to the reality of a harder swim in non-sea waters.

With another hot and sunny day in Yambol, I knew there would be other swimmers in the pool late in the day. I was right as kids were mucking around in the outer lanes with other more sensible and mature swimmers using the middle lanes. It was back to sharing lanes again. I chose a lane with another male swimmer just getting on with business doing mileage with a technically sound and economic front crawl stroke.

As I joined the swimmer, we automatically chose to take the right-hand side of the lane to pass each other, just like the traffic on the roads. The session began with a couple of lengths of breaststroke. It was unnerving each time we passed each other, not so much for the first couple of warm-up lengths, but subsequently stretches once into front crawl mode. Somehow it didn't affect his swim as he continued with his elegant strokes gliding gracefully through the waters like a dolphin. Then there was me with increasing tension leading up to the pass each time. Hitting the lane divider on my right side rather than risk getting too close to my lane partner often occurred. At least I didn't stop or revert to breaststroke, which is some form of progress I guess. It was still a sense of anxiety felt in every one of those passing situations.

Once the front crawl started, there was no going back as we shared the lane for around 15 minutes. He departed, leaving me less agitated and tense and it was just the kids in the next lane I had to contend with now. They were playing around sitting on the lane divider, then diving under it into my swim space and actually underneath me as I swam past. What can you do in these situations other than carrying on and try to ignore their antics?

After each length, it was clear the swim was at best inconsistent. Unless I concentrated on relaxing and gliding fully, it just didn't happen. There was a re-focus many times trying to get the relaxed state back. The longer the swim went on the frequency, trying to purge a relaxed style increased.

I knew whether I was swimming efficiently just by how it felt, but there was another factor by counting the number of stroke cycles it took to swim each length. Having discovered this in a previous session, I had not used this assessing method until today. Now I count the strokes on each length was taken up regularly. Ten strokes and the swim efficiency is good. When it goes up to 11 or 12, I need to re-focus to try and relax again. I could easily predict how many strokes it would take from one end to the other by how I felt in any case and won that little mind game most times.

With all swimmers out of the pool bar one, it was a push to get as many lengths of front crawl in as possible. When the last person got out of the pool leaving me alone, I knew that I had paid to swim for an hour and this length of time had elapsed a while ago. I don't think they mind swimmers being over the hour here after all this is Bulgaria and time factors don't mean much. However, being English, there is a sense of guilt that if felt straight away once going beyond that hour mark. At this point, my short-sightedness meant I had no idea what the actual time was not being able to see the clock without stopping the swim to get nearer. I wanted to carry on just to see how long I could sustain the swim, but the English in me was too much to ignore as I felt compelled to end the session and did so with a couple of sprint lengths to finish. There was no breaststroke used in the main chunk of this swimming session today which was a good omen.

Looking at the clock out now out of the pool, it was now 17:55 - I had been swimming non-stop for 1 hour 10 minutes. The recent sea swim was longer, but freshwater takes more effort. Although the nerves and panic still hit me whenever getting near to other swimmers, it is ideal to have this happening regularly in the pool to try and deal with it.

I don't know how it would feel if the time doubled swimming today. There is always the breaststroke and using the tow float to rest on if it is all too much. Is that cheating?

Things have changed. Just completing the 2-mile course is now not enough. The revised challenge is to do it non-stop and with a wetsuit surely that is now possible. Or is a wetsuit cheating?

One concern still apparent is not having tried out the wetsuit other than a quick 10-minute session in seawater. I think I will have to try it out in the swimming pool one day regardless of the particular strange looks I will get. Maybe the next session planned for Thursday. What the hell!

All in all, at this stage, an hour isn't enough in the pool. It closes at 18:00 and is too busy with kids before 17:00, so no options to extend that the time with this. Another session could be pushed for in the sea before the event; I may consider that.

It was looking good now and more than anything I can't wait to complete the challenge fast approaching, knock swimming on the head and get back onto terra firma with my bike.

Wetsuit with Issues

Today as planned, I was going to be in the school swimming pool donning a wetsuit. With only one fleeting moment in the sea wearing it, this was no real test as to how the swim would feel in freshwater.

The wetsuit has been with me since May, but I have only tried it on twice before this week. The main reason for that was the intense heat we have here in Bulgaria throughout the summer. Yesterday it was put on for the third time, but on my own and I couldn't zip it up at the back. The heat caused profuse sweating directly the wetsuit rose above my waist. I knew from the start this wetsuit was too small for me and therefore a tight fit, but there weren't options to change it from both logistic and financial barriers. The only remedy was to lose a little weight which I'd done over the last few months, but not enough. Losing weight is fine, but losing bulk is another issue. While losing weight, my muscles had developed through that process through a pretty strict fitness regime that had been set up and practised. So although I am down on weight a little, my mass hadn't reduced. Also, as muscle is denser than fat, the former 'bulk' man had now transformed into the 'hulk' man. With this remains the struggle to squeeze into this giant black condom.

There was a cunning plan made up to get into the swimming pool without having to change into the wetsuit in the school changing rooms. It was a calamity trying to put this skin on. It would undoubtedly amuse quite a few onlookers if they saw me attempting that process in the changing rooms. Using plastic bags on my legs initially and gardening gloves to engineer the dressing into position on the arms and legs is bordering on the surreal. Those who have worn wetsuits know what mean here.

The idea was to get the wetsuit on at home and then slip into a pair of shorts. Then add a t-shirt covering the bulk of the wetsuit. With this outfit, a bicycle ride made to the pool as walking in the heat would cause severe sweating and I'd probably have fainted by the time I got there. Another advantage of using the bike was that road to the school was mainly sloping downhill; therefore free-wheeling possible. Also, there is always a breeze in your face when moving on a bike—a great plan.

As the wetsuit struggled on in a semi-strangled fashion, the inevitable sweating started. With open windows, doors and a steady cool breeze running through that channel, there was no relief from the heat generated in this outfit. My attempts made to zip-up and complete the seal was successful this time, but only after a bit of coaxing, cursing and countless re-runs of the zip movements up and down. It felt like I had just been through a sausage skinning machine with hiccups! Yes, it was tight, but touching my toes and stretching my arms wasn't too much of a problem with the stretchability of the neoprene material. There was, however, an unnerving fear of hearing a sudden rip in the process. It does take a little extra effort moving around and I imagine this would be the same when moving body parts in swimming mode.

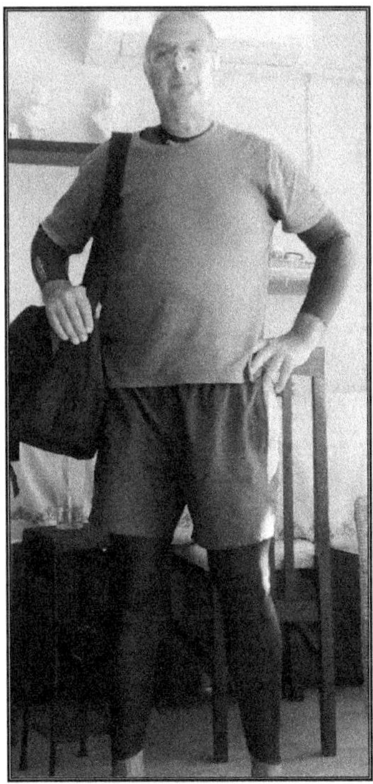

Hiding a Wetsuit

Shorts and t-shirt on and it was on my bike rolling down the road to the pool. In my keenness, I arrived a little earlier than usual, so I paused a while at a traffic crossroad junction en route. There was a breeze to cool me down at this location caused by traffic zooming past me. Five minutes of ventilation and I was on my way again arriving at the pool site in no time.

When I got there, I just couldn't wait to get in the water with the intense heat that had built up and was still transmitting from inside the wetsuit. I felt drips of sweating running down my back and my forehead riddled with pores streaming out sweat that teamed up into a mini fountain running down my face.

Where was the receptionist when I got there? Had she gone absent without leave? The Lifeguard saw me arrive and kindly offered to call the receptionist telling her I was waiting. The last thing I needed was waiting in a non-ventilated reception room sweating for England with no option other than to wait and drip sweat all over the floor. It was a full 10 minutes before someone came to take my 3 leva and present me with a ticket to swim. It couldn't come too soon as I squeaked with an internal slush of sweat into the changing room.

It was off with the shorts and t-shirt and a quick swap of my prescription glasses for goggles. With earplugs in, the cap on there was no hesitation going straight into the shower. It was a cold shower where I anticipated a great relief from the heat. But with this wetsuit on surprisingly, I couldn't feel any of the coolness of the cold water. It was like a fire that wouldn't extinguish.

The impatience of getting into the pool water was too much as I skipped the stretching exercises and directly entered the pool. Only one person was using a lane, so I had a choice of three and opted for one in the centre. Because of the delay, it was now 16:55, but that didn't bother me as this was a test for the wetsuit today, not the usual swimming endurance session.

Once starting the swim with breaststroke, a familiar problem returned. My legs were kicking air again with the extra buoyancy of the wetsuit. It was a more strenuous effort needed with my downward arm strokes to raise my head. The issues here were the same experience that was found in that short spell trying the suit out in the sea. It wasn't a comfortable or relaxed feeling, but I persevered for four lengths to see whether I could adapt. My stroke gradually became shorter and there was no other alternative technique I could use that would give way to using less effort. Wasting masses of energy trying to keep my legs underwater was strange. When not wearing a wetsuit the primary energy needed in the arms was for headway not forcing my legs down. I wasn't happy with this, but then there is always front crawl to rely on with this wetsuit.

Into the front crawl and after the first few strokes, the signs were good. It was also my intention to try a couple of random right-side breathing attempts during this test session. I attempted this on my first length and I wished I hadn't as suddenly a great panic set in straight away - as always. My reaction was to try again as I was annoyed, but the consequences this time it was even worse. Even though I returned to left side breathing straight away to try and recover, this was a shock to the system and my confidence died. Still, I tried again thinking it couldn't get any worse, but it was all too much and my feet reached for the bottom of the pool for the first time in ages!

I was in a mess at this point and it felt like I was suffocating from all angles. This suffocation exaggerated wearing a wetsuit and an unpleasant, almost unbearable moment. At this point, I wanted to be freed from all the anxiety of swimming, mummification and give up this seemingly ridiculous lark.

With the 2-mile event fast approaching, in fact, in two weeks, was this event now out of my reach in a wetsuit? Could I cope with the cold London waters without a wetsuit after blessed with a heated pool and warm sea waters to date?

My mind was now adjusted and reset just to do what I had done before for countless hours and sensible thinking was in play. A pause for thought made and the recall of online advice when swimmers get into this kind of state. That wetsuit scientifically makes it easier to swim and aids the breathing technique significantly. Subsequently armed with more information, it made complete sense to don the wetsuit and completely give up trying to breathe on the right side forever!

Here we go again after a pause and sensible reflection. The front crawl starts up again with left side breathing only. 55 minutes later it was the end of the session - time up. Yes, it does take up a little more effort with the resistance of the tightness of the wetsuit, but there are so many other positive benefits. Whereas I took a minimum of 10-stroke cycles to do a length with proper technique without a wetsuit, this went down to 9 with the outfit. There is no effort needed in leg kicks to keep the body level in the water. With this, rather than being lazy with no effort with leg kicks, now sporadic kicking was made to give more forward movement rather than just for balance. Breathing, (to the left) was more comfortable with a slightly raised front end and head. I now had to force my head down under the water to get a more streamlined body. Before this, I was pushing my head up to breath with extra effort with the left arm stroke. Overall, there was less energy needed with the wetsuit.

A 55-minute swim and I could have gone on for much longer. At this point, I would still prefer to swim without a wetsuit now knowing the difference from the first-hand experience. However, this is the first time in freshwater and the sensible option is to give it another go, but don't go doing stressful things such as right side breathing.

During that 55 minutes of front crawl, I did put in two lengths of breaststroke just out of curiosity. It didn't feel like it was a recovery stroke and it stressed me out a bit with the awkwardness of the stroke in a wetsuit. My idea now is if a break or pause needed, either use the tow float which will be with me or just turn and float on my back. These ploys will give the necessary assurances required in times of panic replacing breaststroke.

The only question now is what stroke to start with in the event? Considering there will be with hundreds of other swimmers splashing about and on each other what do I do? Seemingly breaststroke is now out of the equation with a wetsuit. I will continue to persevere with breaststroke to try and solve that issue in the meantime.

Into the shower, wetsuit stripped off and the opportunity to get it washed there and then. It was a massive relief to get out of that skin and I felt wholly liberated after being tight enveloped for two and a half hours.

Back home, the wetsuit drip-dried hanging out on our apartment balcony for all the neighbourhood to see. Strangely, there was something quite special and unique about that bit of washing hanging out in public.

Going Through the Motions

It was a morning of harvesting sweetcorn and uprooting the stems that had dried out over the last few weeks. This produce was food for my neighbour's rabbits in the winter and I knackered by lunchtime. As I loaded the rabbit feed into the car boot, I jarred my left knee in the process. Not long after, my knee swelled up and became painful. It was a good job there wasn't cycling or running waiting for me in the afternoon with this.

Fleeting moments were succumbing with temptations hard to resist a fresh apple from the tree, just like the original Adam. Added to this were a few juicy ripe figs and succulent sweet grapes that just called out to feast on. Unlike Adam and the apple, no fig leaves over my private parts in this story. There was a little nervy feeling after eating the fruit, especially with the consequences experienced the previous fruit feast before training. This time though it wasn't such a glutinous occasion.

Even though my wetsuit was too small, once on it is forgotten and I just got on with things. The sizing issue means it takes nearly 20 minutes to put on. The bulk of the time taken up was trying to ride the material up and around my torso, giving more slack needed for the zip to ride up at the back. The zip finally made it after a good 10 minutes of frustrating tinkering, cursing and extreme sweating. It was too late to get a better fitting wetsuit and even if I had finances to hand; outfits are scant here in Bulgaria. This wetsuit will just have to make do. Only a week and a half to go to the event in any case.

It was an action replay of the previous session with the wetsuit semi-disguised under scant summer clothing. And blow me down with a feather, would you believe it another 10-minute wait at the reception for the cashier to turn up again. This event was something I would have put good money on never to happen again even though I'm not a gambling man. Over the last six months, since I had been coming here, this had never happened before. Now, twice in the row! I stood by the entrance door in a vain search for a trace of a breeze.

At this stage dehydration was inevitable, not just from sweating wearing the wetsuit, but from this morning's graft on the farm with the only liquid taken on was a cup of tea and a cup of coffee during the day. My mind was positive with a view that dehydration may well be the case after 90 minutes of swimming in the London event. It would be useful to experience and practice how it felt swimming while in a dehydrated state.

The pool finally greeted me in at 16:45. There was an opportunity to get more than an hour of freestyle in with the pool now virtually empty. This freedom was probably because school children have started their summer break this week, which means I get a welcome break from the children! With this in mind, next Thursday, I will be able to turn up earlier without fear of being hindered by juvenile junctions. Perhaps there might even be an opportunity to pay for two hours in the pool and use that time to have a run at the 2-mile distance.

Today, however, once in the pool it was eight lengths of breaststroke trying to get the legs to push water rather than air. Without a wetsuit, breaststroke is snail's pace. With a wetsuit, it slows down to half a snail's pace! Restricted arm strokes with the tightness of the wetsuit didn't help and just like last time, it was an effort working on the arms, which meant I couldn't maintain it for very long.

It was good now to get into the front crawl, almost a relief. Now that's something I'd never thought I'd say a few weeks ago. During the monotonous up and down lengths, there were challenges set to keep me focused. The main target was to see whether I could reduce the number of stroke cycles for each length. The norm was 9, but a few times, I got it down to 8 and on one occasion 7. The reason this was possible was to focus on gliding more and therefore delay the stroke. In a wetsuit, you can delay more as there is a tendency to drift forward rather than sink. Also, there is a significant difference in the overall speed attained motion. This newly acquired technique in a wetsuit was great motivator giving rise to little more power in the strokes and see it directly convert into faster forward motion.

Not having to focus on basic swimming techniques now, I was now looked to further experiment for the most effective position of the stroke pull underwater. Also, more attention using my body to turn with my head rather than just swivelling my head. This tactic used less energy and gave a more streamlined position. However, I can achieve this if relaxed. I was now buzzing each time I reached the end of a length seeing the pool floor move quickly beneath me and the pool walls each end when sighting, speeding towards me. I never thought I would ever get to this stage.

There was another young teenage female swimmer in the next lane also doing front crawl. Naturally, I compared it with my own. Another ego boost was when I sped past her on many occasions without any effort. Yes, I was in a wetsuit and subconsciously maybe put a little more effort. She stopped for a breather every length whereas I just carried on without pausing. The swim timed out at over 1 hour and 5 minutes by the time I quit.

During that time in the water, after 45 minutes cramp shot into my left calf muscle, a change of position with my leg action got rid of that. A little later there was a more severe bout of cramp in my right thigh. Getting rid of that took a bit more work. The consequence here was dehydration as I anticipated and please it was dealt with without stopping.

There were moments where I did feel some anxiety during this swim. These moments were brought on mainly with the thought of not having ever been in open freshwater swimming environment since I nearly drowned all those years ago. School pools and small hotel pools are nothing like open water. With heated water, not being subjected to bad weather and always a few seconds pause after every length to turn, there would be no such luxury in open waters. Also, swimming blind freestyle is okay with a lane free, but what if clashes occur with other swimmers? How would I react to being ducked or battered?

There were also many phases in the swim where it felt like I had indigestion. It comes and goes without warning. These moments only last a few minutes and I wasn't too sure what causes this. I don't usually eat in the afternoon and the same was the case today, so maybe that was the problem. The stomach is trying to digest something that isn't there. With the London event in the morning and breakfast some two to three hours earlier that indigestion issue, fingers crossed this won't happen. Regardless of any anxiety, indigestion or any other medical problem, there is always going to be that safety tow float to hug and recover.

All done and dusted and back home it was into the usual sequence of plank routines. My left knee was still feeling the pain from the jarring this morning. There was some distinct discomfort in the plank routine lifting my right leg which causes my left leg supporting the whole of my body. I hope it will repair itself quickly as I am up to an 18-minute session now and want to target 20 minutes by Monday. Sweat was still pouring out of me during this session, so no real concerns of being severely dehydrated.

If I'm honest I have to admit this evening I was a little tired but from the events of the whole day not just from swimming. There are not too many concerns now that I have the technique to complete the 2-mile event in front crawl. However, you never know what is in store on the day.

Paradoxically, No Sweat Today

The aim today was to take the opportunity to get more non-stop swimming time during the last few training sessions. With kids finished in school for the summer and away from the pool, there was the chance to turn up earlier and get more uninterrupted minutes in.

So it was on with the wetsuit and disguise toppings at home. Then down the stairs with my bike and on my way for an earlier and longer session. As I reached the bottom of the stairs, I met with a different set of stairs. These were stares from a neighbour who saw me about to mount the bike sweating profusely before I'd even started pedalling off. We greeted each other and spoke for a while. She thought I was wearing the wetsuit to lose weight by sweating and didn't consider I was going swimming, naturally. I didn't have the patience or inclination to explain as time was ticking away with more sweat seeping from my flooding pores and running amok inside this outfit.

There was no waiting for the receptionist today. Thank God! As I passed through, I was surprised to see children drying their hair on free hairdryers on the wall of the reception area. Above the din of the hairdryers, my fee was paid and straight into the changing rooms to meet two other guys who had also just arrived. It was 16:10 and I had an empty lane in the pool by 16:20 just as predicted. My thoughts were on the potential time I now had free to swim. After a short calculation, it worked out to be around an hour and a half.

After four lengths of breaststroke, there was some success trying to keep my legs underwater, but I didn't dwell. It was into the front crawl with the intent of longevity.

During the whole time, my lane was clear and noticeably avoided by other swimmers who entered the pool. It had to be due to my swimming in a wetsuit and solely on my own. I guess it gave an air of importance and a deterrent for swimmers who saw this and avoided joining me. Also, because I didn't rest or stop throughout the time in the water, they must have thought I was on a mission. Well, they were right. The creation of an 'air of importance' was another unexpected bonus of wearing a wetsuit in a heated swimming pool.

As usual, the mood of swim goes through phases. The longer the time swimming, the harder it is to keep good form and technique. There were no issues with water filling up my sinuses today. It was the first time this hadn't plagued me and I hadn't a clue as to why it suddenly stopped.

The number of stroke cycles for each length was pretty constant. It varied from 8 to 9 with an occasional 9½, which was a reminder to re-focus on the style and technique. This refocussing invariably brought the number of stroke cycles down to 8 on next length.

For the first time, there was a problem with my black Bulgarian swimming cap which I had been wearing it for each swim unfailingly for six months. After around 40 minutes it was at the point of slipping off. The dislodging happened on several occasions and had to be pulled back down on each occasion. Maybe it was because the rubber was getting old and more flimsy over the number of times worn. Or and here's a thought, perhaps because of the increased swimming speed which may have forced it to slip back. There are only two sessions to go now before the event with a new cap provided, so no real need to replace it at this stage.

Having now swum for an hour, it was now just me in the pool. The lifeguard strutting around the pool with her body language saying, 'Hurry up I want to go home!'. A sense of guilt carried with me over me the next fifteen minutes. I interpreted this as a form of bullying, so I didn't enjoy that mentally.

I had already gone past the hour that I'd paid adding substantially to the uncomfortable guilty feeling of carrying on with just me in the pool. Sometimes I wish I could get rid of that essential British trait. Guilt wouldn't have ever entered into any Bulgarian head put into the same situation.

The swim today lasted 1 hour 15 minutes but could have quite easily gone on for much longer. I had worked out that each length takes around 30 seconds. Thirty seconds for each 17-metre length and the overall time worked out with a little maths. At this pace, the 2-mile Serpentine event distance should take a smidgen over 90 minutes. I was quite amazed that potentially this swim could be done at this time. It is a more robust open water environment, but then I don't stop and start to turn around every 30 seconds so that should balance itself out.

With the event fast approaching, my estimated time for completing the 2-mile event was initially 3 hours using breaststroke with sporadic front crawl. This predicted time has now halved with the new approach in training. Having said that I would still be more than happy to complete the event in less than 2 hours.

Another ploy I tried today was to try and get rid of that indigestion problem when swimming. I'm sure it happens because I hadn't eaten since breakfast which was getting on close to 10 hours. Just as an experiment, I made a cheese sandwich and ate washed down with a glass of cold milk two hours before the swim started. This tasty tactic seemed to work very well with no issues at all with indigestion or other internal acid-based discomforts. So now I know what to do in the next training session and it doesn't involve starving myself. Luckily the event won't need such provision as it is in the morning.

Back home it was 19 minutes of plank exercises and well on course for the 20-minute target next Monday. It was, however, a great struggle for me to do the planking today. The pain barriers I go through on this are incredible. The thought of putting myself through this torture doesn't motivate. I could have quite easily given it a miss today. It was only the thought of how angry I would be with myself if I skipped it.

At lunchtime today, my weight was 82.2 kilograms. By the end of the training session, this had gone down to 80.2 kilograms. That loss was purely through fluid loss.

No sea swimming this weekend as chores are crying out on the farm. So the next swim was now planned for next Tuesday. There is a temptation to take a chance and get an extra one in on Monday regardless of the potential 'Monday blues' factor.

Angry Today – With Myself!

This session is the last swim pushing myself with training. The reason was, with only four days to go to the event, whatever I do after today won't make much difference to my fitness and readiness. Pushing too hard will probably just wear me out for the big day. So after this session, it will be a well-deserved winding down to the event. There was no distraction from the work to be done today as I turned up at the pool knowing that shortly, the swimming adventure was finally coming to an end.

Getting into my wetsuit at home was a nightmare. It took a full 20 minutes to get into it. I spent most of that time trying to do that blessed zip up at the back. It seemed a hopeless cause for ages trying to self-zip myself. I was frustrated cursing under my breath for my weak resolve for not losing more weight as I had planned. Trying to lose weight here is like fighting against a powerful tide of wholesome luxurious food and drink. With the issues of dressing up this wetsuit, it felt like I'd actual bulked up and put on more weight over the last five days!

After jumping up and down and doing Houdini style contortions, I finally sealed the wetsuit. I was a human Niagara Falls of sweat from all the efforts that were involved with the task. Finally, freewheeling my bike to the pool donning the usual t-shirt, shorts and very much relieved.

Today is around 32C in Yambol with a forceful sun beating down on the way to the school pool. Sweat was dripping off from all points of my body that overhung. As I made my way past many school children who were hanging around, they must have wondered why I am drenched.

It was 16:05 and I had visions of getting at least 90 minutes swimming in on this session. The receptionist was busy, so a little wait was on. The sweat was building up further while waiting for her to attend to my needs. When she finally did get to me, she put her hand up, showing five. Funny how she doesn't speak to me. I understand her when she does speak, but she decided to show me a 'high five' this time without words. I replied with a silent okay by giving a thumbs up and went back outside with school kids playing in the playground. I thought it was their summer break and couldn't understand why they were still attending until I asked. I found out that it was only the younger children who had broken up for the summer at this point.

I settled down on the steps leading up the entrance and recalled my days as a school kid with the thought that five minutes wasn't a long time to wait. Sitting down with my hands resting on my knees, a stream of sweat running down my arm. Then rolling down my fingers finally dripped onto the steps below where I was sitting. After a few minutes, a large pool of sweat that gathered cascaded down from one step down to the other. I couldn't ever recall sweating as much as this before, even in a sauna! As I put my hands together and positioned more sweat began to run from my nose to drop in the same spot, I felt like a human distillery. It was just like wine distilled into rakia with the same rate of liquid dripping out. This constant stream of sweat continued as the time ticked on for what I know was much longer than five minutes.

After about fifteen minutes, I went back to the reception area and asked if the pool was ready yet. Once again, the hand went up, showing me a 'high five'. I was not a bundle of joy with this mysterious Bulgarian five minutes. It has now tripled! Well, I knew she was bound to call me when the pool was ready.

Half an hour later still wearing a wetsuit drenched with sweat from the inside the sweat now permutated to the outer area. The suit now had many areas of white powdered salt stains from perforated sweat that had seeped through and evaporated. There was still no call-up! I was now angry as I went in and asked what the problem was. She finally spoke to me and seeing I was irate and soaked gave me the okay to go in. I didn't bother thanking her, unlike me, as I was now rushing everything. I showered the salt stains off the wetsuit and prepared to swim.

As I entered the pool area, some 20 young children under instruction using all the lanes. This kid crowd must have been the start of summer school swimming lessons. As one of the swimming instructors saw this dark wet-suited figure approach, she told the children in the far lane to move over giving up that lane for me. It was now 16:55. I had been stuck in that wetsuit in the stifling Bulgarian summer heat for over 50 minutes! Only then did it click - Oh fool me! When the receptionist showed me the 'high five, she didn't mean five minutes but signalled five o'clock! If only she had told me and not showed me I would have understood. I was angry with myself for not realising this.

Finally, it was into the waters and four lengths of breaststroke and then straight into non-stop front crawl finishing just over an hour later when the time was up.

It wasn't a particularly useful session in terms of technique. I was trying to get some sighting in which disrupts the regular rhythm of the stroke. I know this is necessary for the event with so many people around. My mind was on these potential issues in the Serpentine throughout the session. The wondering focussed on the differences and probable problems that I might have to face soon in open waters compared to the calmness of pool swimming. In reality, have had no experience in the open water swimming or for that matter swimming alongside other swimmers. I was under no illusions and fully aware that other people swimming near me would be the main issue. Also, I'd only used the tow float on only one occasion and without a wetsuit. I couldn't see that presenting a problem unless there is a strong tailwind and it gets in the way of the front crawl stroke as it did at sea. All these things were going through my mind during this session. A positive factor was that I could have gone on for much longer without a delayed start.

Well, that's another visit to the pool out of the way; one more to go! The last swim was planned on Thursday and will be without the wetsuit so I can just relax and take it easy in that final session.

Home again and 21 minutes of plank exercises practised. I did plan to get to 20 minutes in by Monday but achieved that last Saturday. That's where it stops now as the winding down starts for the swimming event at the weekend.

The Last Practice Session?

The plan today was to just have a leisurely swim without the hassle of the wetsuit and maybe finish early. So, did my intentions go to plan today?

No, I decided not to go training at the last moment! Whatever I did in the pool today, it wouldn't make any difference to what happens Saturday. Besides which, I felt tired and worn-out more mentally than physically after all this time. I just wanted to complete the event and take a little rest bite from training. With the event taking place in less than 48 hours, I am more concerned with the travelling logistics to London.

40 Ticket Receipts Collected

So, no swimming session today and I can't see me returning to the pool again after the swim in London. I still can't believe how fortunate it has been to have access to a pool so close to my home added to which the nominal entry fee charged. I know there had been 40 swimming sessions as I had collected all the receipts for each visit. The total cost of those 40 swimming sessions in the school pool over the last 6-month period was 120 leva. Yes, there were issues with kids, timings and closures, but all this is water under the bridge now.

The start of the journey to London was a car drive of some 300 kilometres from my home town Yambol to the airport in Bulgaria's capital city Sofia. I needed to start very early in the morning as the flight leaves Sofia at 12:05. Having looked at all other public transport options, I can only say it would be dodgy at the very least knowing how these work here in Bulgaria. Trains and coaches are cheap, but no guarantees of arriving on time or even turning up for that matter. A taxi is far too expensive, therefore getting there under my own steam in my car was the best choice therefore the fate of travel would in my own hands.

It had been a nightmare trying to book a parking space for my car near Sofia Airport. The system requires having a third party bank account to pay before you can book. The registration for this includes an intensive security process, including a profile picture and an identification document. All these had to be scanned and downloaded to their website. It took two days before the process was complete before I could finally book a parking space with confirmation to hand. An unnecessary pig's ear of a system and yet another hurdle to negotiate!

Once the plane lands in the UK three and a half hours later, it was a coach ride from Stanstead Airport to Victoria, London. The place I am staying overnight is around an hour walking distance from Victoria Coach Station, so no further costs on public transport needed in London. Besides which, I looked forward to stretching my legs with a walk after being seated most of the day on the plane and coach.

Because I live abroad, the Serpentine event pack with all the mandatory gear to be worn such as number, wristband and an official cap could not be posted to me. I have to pick these up on the day of the event at Serpentine Information Centre tent one hour before the start. I just hope the official swimming cap fits. To my relief there will be many people who I could ask to come to my rescue and zip up my wetsuit at the back; a bonus there then!

Then there are the Serpentine swim event pictures, which were offered at half price if booked in advance before the day of the event. Yet again, because I live abroad and naturally don't have a UK postcode linked with any of my bank accounts, I couldn't technically pay for the picture bundle. Yey again, hurdles put in front of me. To be fair, the company that is taking the pictures have been helpful, but unfortunately still leaving me helpless. All they could suggest was to get someone in the UK to pay on my behalf. Again, masses of time was needed to organise this. Four days and counting and they were still not booked up with a deadline of 24 hours before the discount date expires. It was finally trusted to and sorted out by my youngest son Nathan in the UK, so eventually one less worry.

Then there was bloody Ryanair and anyone that has ever flown with them hates them. They have to be the worst budget airline going and fully justified. But I, like hundreds of thousands of others had no choice given the monopoly they had on destinations required

Booking in with Ryan Air was fine going out to the UK. Then their stupid games began to suck money out of you. They tactically ask you to pay extra to reserve a seat for the return trip as this is the only way to check in more than 24 hours before the due flight. They know that most passengers do not have a printer in their holiday suitcase and don't want the inconvenience of having to get a boarding pass printed out from another source abroad. Oh, and 50 Euros charge if a boarding pass not presented! I, therefore, had to pay a fee to reserve my seat and am left feeling very bitter about that. This dastardly ploy was bordering on the side of criminality! I might add that I am not in the least surprised with their snide policies from past experiences with them.

Travelling light is the name of the game tomorrow, not just because of the want, but because of Ryanair's measly free baggage allowance. Just enough space for a wetsuit, a deflated tow float - not even space for a towel.

These hurdles straddled but more ahead. Even trying to print out the coach ticket for the return trip from Stanstead to Victoria Coach Station took two days to sort out. With the long summer season and the heat here, my printer cartridge dried up and I had to get a refill before it could print out.

All I have been saying to myself over the last week is, 'Nothing's Easy!'

The only thing that went to plan was the booking of a room near Hyde Park for one night. This reservation made some six months ago as there may not have been vacant places on a low budget if booked later in the year. Pat on the back for that.

With almost all hurdles now out of the way, I hoped that all the work put in over the last six months was going to be worth it. The swimming was something I didn't enjoy, but the challenge was, which for many months I thought was not achievable. No matter what, I will complete the 2-mile swim with a sunny and warm day forecast in London.

Six months of training was now in the bank and it was the time of reckoning. But I was still in Yambol and the show was over 3000 kilometres away in my former home city of London.

There was a slight change of plan, as I was going to be accompanied by Galia's nephew Tedi on the drive to Sofia. Brought up in Yambol, he like many others now attends a big city University in Sofia. After the summer break with family and girlfriend Ilina who is still studying at college in Yambol, he was now due to return to Sofia for the new University term this weekend. He will help me to stay awake on the drive as I know he is good company and loves practising his English with me so we will be incessant talking throughout the trip.

The alarm rang out at 03:50 only to find that it was pouring with rain. Yesterday I thoroughly cleaned the car ready for the trip and got it into my garage just before it surprisingly started to rain. There was no forecast for rain when I checked the day before. Why do I bother? Well, at least it is clean rain here.

Trying to find Tedi's home on the outskirts of Yambol in pitch darkness was difficult. The streets were unlit and confusion compounded with pouring rain that had filled all potholes that randomly scattered the streets. The water had disguised the depth of the potholes and a high risk now running blindly into them. The last thing I wanted was to become a non-starter on this trip with damaged wheels on the car. A slower and more wary drive was needed and made a little easier devoid of other traffic up my proverbial backside bullying me for more speed.

Once Tedi was gathered, we were on our way heading 300 kilometres due west. It was intense amounts of concentration needed to drive in these conditions with seemingly countless lorries churning out blinding spray from the rain. It was shocking to witness how many commercial trucks only had one backlight working! We chatted non-stop throughout the whole journey as expected with two stops for coffee and a cigarette for Tedi.

With only 10 kilometres to go, the rain had just about cleared and daylight had secretly crept upon us with no sunrise due to rain cloud cover. Tedi was dropped off at a Metro train station after a hug and best wishes as we went our separate ways. I felt quite sad seeing him go and wished he was coming with me as we get on so well. He became inspired by my adventure and may have intentions of such a challenge with me next year. I might mention again that this is not usual for Bulgarians; they usually want the easiest and relaxed life avoiding setting themselves unnecessary burdens.

Having parked my car in an Ibis Hotel car park then board a van giving a shuttle service to the airport some two kilometres away. It was a 30-minute wait before the van arrived. I could have walked there within that time, but with temperatures steadily rising it wasn't wise considering the surplus amount of clothing I was wearing.

My allocated seat on the plane was the furthest to the front on the left with a window view. Strangely enough, my return seat was the last seat at the back on the right with a window view! What are the chances of that happening again? There was no risk of me falling asleep on plane trips, especially this one being right next to the busy flight attendants trying their best to catering and ripping off herds of travellers with extortionately priced beverages.

The flight only took 2 hours 50 minutes with a tailwind arriving some 20 minutes earlier than scheduled. So far, so good.

The National Express coach was waiting for me in the allocated bay as I edged my way through thousands of other passengers returning from holidays. I've never seen such crowds in an airport before. Maybe because I had never had a holiday at the height of the holiday season and this was the tail end of the high season. I couldn't imagine for a moment how this airport would manage with greater crowds in August!

There was one thing I liked about National Express coaches and that was the comfortable seats they have. The journey was enjoyable, watching all the increasing commotion outside in the comfort of the coach as we neared and entered London. I was so glad I don't live there anymore. At this point, I just wanted to get to our destination, do the event and get out as soon as possible. The only things I was looking forward to in London was the traffic-free Hyde Park and the medals after the swim.

After arriving in London's Victoria coach station is was a 4-kilometre walk to my booked accommodation. My baggage was a six-year-old crumpled and faded Asda shopping bag held together with an old plastic belt. This was carried under my arm. I was hot and for a good reason as I was wearing a double layer of clothing to save on baggage weight. It was off with one of the pairs of socks and a shirt leaving a single layer of clothing to try and reduce insulation. I was still wearing two sets of underpants not wanting to get arrested for indecency taking one pair off in public.

Headway made and Hyde Park arrived, which was coincidentally on the way to the accommodation booked. There was a hive of activity around the Serpentine Lake area. All the main event structures up and many helpers were picking up dead leaves that had fallen over the last few days. It was quite exciting knowing that in the morning, this area will be swarming with swimmers and at with very least one recent non-swimmer. I didn't dwell, plenty of time tomorrow to do that and it was back walking on towards my accommodation.

As airline regulations restrict travellers from taking homemade food in their hand luggage I was now forced to shop for food having not eaten since breakfast in Yambol. It was a nervy mind contemplating a meal in a bar or restaurant on two points. Firstly, this was not my regular healthy diet leading to inevitable stomach issues later and secondly the ridiculous cost, which would ruin my appetite.

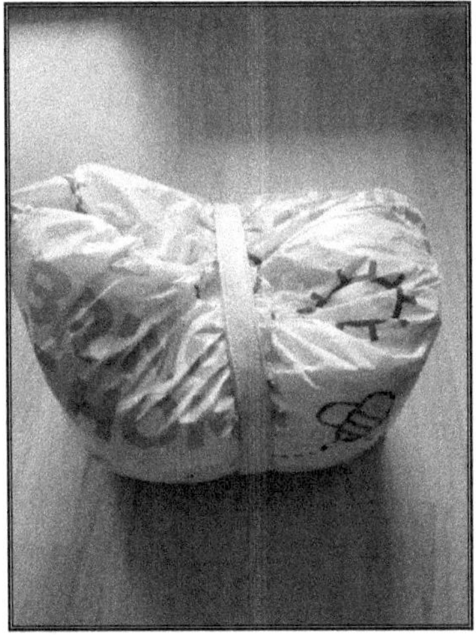

My Only Luggage, an Old Asda Bag

I booked in at the accommodation some 13 hours 30 minutes after leaving my home in Yambol and found that my room was on the 4th Floor with 50 steps leading up to it. There was no early breakfast available at these digs before 07:00, so I had told the landlord I'd provide my own as I would have checked out by this time. He was well pleased with that and shook my hand to show his gratitude and thanks. There was more than a glint of money lit up in his eyes once the suggestion announced.

Up all those creaking stairs to the room then revealing the digs were in close similarity to a rabbit hutch. No matter, as long as it had a bed and a private toilet that was okay. The shower dripped water with the tap full on with a severely fractured shower base, again no matter. At least the drips of water were warm, but then even the cold water taps expelled warm water in this place! No fridge, so the purchased carton of milk for the morning sat in the sink in the bathroom overnight as the ceramic material made this the coolest place.

My evening meal from Sainsbury's consisted of a mayonnaise swamped bacon pasta, chicken, (I think) and vegetable wrap with prepared fruit for dessert. I had to laugh at myself thinking of the 'best before' date on the package. It would be more truthful to replace this with 'best before eating'. This chemical-laden food was in complete contrast to my healthy meals and snacks in Bulgaria. The amount of plastic wrapping used with these goods that were trying to straighten itself back up and climb out of the waste bin was criminal. Why so much plastic used is beyond me. With the knowledge and technology we have, it shouldn't be an issue. I knew there would be issues with all the food here not being able to replicate my sustained regular chemical-free diet. I daren't read the ingredients before, (or after) I ate it as this would just play horror games in my head overnight. Funny how we eat numbers detailed and listed on the back of the packet. The only numbers I was concerned with was the subsequent number ones and number twos overnight and in the morning!

'Rabbit Hutch' Accommodation, but Comfy Bed

There was no Wi-Fi signal here either for reasons seemingly as this room was the furthest away from the reception where the source of the signal is. With that, there was no chance of telling Galia I'm okay which has been the case all day. Of all the places in the world you would expect a Wi-Fi service in the centre of London, but none!

The bed was the only place to sit in this room. At 21:30 the sitting position was now changed to being a horizontal sleeping position with the alarm set for 06:30. I was more than curious about what tomorrow will hold. I was so glad I had decided to pursue this challenge regardless of the numerous hurdles and other obstacles that had tried their best to put me off. Coming to terms with not following this challenge through by giving up would have been very difficult. Avoiding failure was a big part of the drive that kept it on track. Tomorrow will see how the last hurdles unfold.

Journey's End - The Serpentine 2-mile Swim

During the night, I suffered from leg cramps. The choice made was to dehydrate purposely the day before the swim and this the apparent reason for the night of muscle pains. The dehydrating decision was to reduce toilet trips in the night hopefully aiding an uninterrupted night of sleep. Lack of toilet trips, unfortunately, was not the case at all. That evening saw a pint of English craft beer downed before my evening food, which I thought would enhance dehydration. The beer, good as it was, just compounded further the alien diet this weekend. That evening my stomach began to make noises like it had started a swimming event well before the Serpentine Lake swim was due. With gurgling and splashing sounds within, the digestions system didn't sound too healthy and a big worry to carry into the next day!

Later that night there were interruptions with other guests tramping up and down the creaking stairs and slamming doors to at 2:30 in the morning after returning from their night out. These were not bad people being vindictive, but just normal sounds made in this accommodation complex as I found earlier climbing up those noisy stairs. After they got into their room, incessant talking began heard through the wafer-thin walls. These were people just talking normally, but against a background of silence and room dividers that might as well not be there, it was as if they were sitting next to me in bed. There were earplugs I could use, but being packed up and embedded in my swimming kit so not easily accessible. Besides which, the fear of not hearing the alarm with earplugs in wasn't an option I wanted to take.

Three lots of toilet trips were still made overnight, despite the pointless efforts made for dehydrating during the day. Getting back to sleep after that last toilet call was difficult and that solitary pint of beer had a lot to answer for and laid the blame there. However, I do recall my doctor saying that the daily prescribed tablets I take for high blood pressure that causes the late-night toilet tours. Lying there wide awake in the middle of the night and through to the early hours of the morning felt strange, almost surreal, but I couldn't quite work out why.

I had previously set the alarm to go off a 06:30, but I was already awake and out of bed at 06:05. When the alarm finally rang out, I was already tucking into my oats and milk with a cup of Black English tea on the side. Not being able to bring my breakfast over in my hand luggage was more than inconvenient. It took ages to try and find something similar in the numerous shops here and ended up with an oat-based porridge type breakfast. I just added milk to it as I couldn't heat it as the instructions said. However, I don't think it makes much difference as it will warm up once in my stomach anyway.

Television is something I don't usually have on or watch when I am on my own. This morning however it was on with the BBC churning out news and going on about something quite obscure and seemingly quite dated. The esoteric topics on the television added to the air of strangeness I felt before in the night. Then a thought occurred - Why was it still dark outside? It was now 06:30 and I knew that sunrise was due at 06:40. As I glanced back at the television and focussed into the bottom left corner of the screen, the time shown was 04:33! Well blow me down with a feather and slap my face with a wet haddock, I hadn't taken into account the two hours' time difference between London and Sofia when setting the alarm. I was now halfway through my breakfast and wide awake. What do I do?

Breakfast now curtailed, a quick brush of the teeth, television off and back to bed after resetting my alarm again for 06:30 GMT. With this man now full of expectation and the enticement of the day ahead, trying to get more sleep was downright impossible. There was no chance of that alarm going off at 06:30 before I rose and started the day again. I just lay there fully conscious of each minute ticking away.

It was 06:00 and with my mind working overtime, the alarm cancelled and the day began again in earnest. I just had to get up and do something to take my mind and body into reality rather than continuing to let vivid oracles continually sweep over me.

My half ate breakfast of oat mix had solidified and the tea now stone cold, but I finished them off anyway. I looked forward to a cup of fresh coffee made to keep me company in the bathroom. No daily book of daily crossword puzzles being solved with me this morning, which is my routine on the throne.

A limp shower, but a shower nonetheless churned out a primed trained athlete that was raring to go. Having shaved my whole body a few days ago, yes I'm a hairy beast, it felt great feeling the trickle of warm water on my skin. How many times in the past body hair ridiculed and assimilated to a gorilla by others? This cruel tease had disturbed and upset me countless times. A plus here for wetsuits which form an excellent disguise for hairy people not forced to shave each time swims take place.

No stomach issues, although the concert sounds of my stomach may well be the overture to problems later. With time to spare and despite previously prepared with due care and attention the night before, I couldn't resist checking and re-checking my kit. I was about to leave the room to free it up for other rabbits. Once that hutch door closed behind me a 'no fixed abode' status hung over me during the next 36 hours up until I arrive back home. A deep sense of contentment belonging to Bulgaria hit in.

Destination - Hyde Park, London

Countless times checking my baggage gave confidence everything for the day ahead now primed and set. Picking up the Asda shopping bag ready to walk out, gurgling in my stomach erupts. This toiletry warning signal caused a short delay before attempting to leave the digs once again and a man slightly lighter than before. Nerves rose again about the toilet issues, but knowing toilet facilities in Hyde Park will be there calmed me down. I hoped my stomach clears before my wetsuit donned.

The walk, on a warm sunny morning, wasn't enjoyed until entering into a traffic-free and reduced noise of Hyde Park. Every other swimmer walking towards the event carried their posh rucksacks, designer sports bags or the supplied kit carrier from the event organisers sent to them by post. Then there was me with my belt wrapped Asda shopping bag. Once again, there is something special about being different from others that stimulate, but then I've always been purposely distanced from the bullying and influence of fashion peddlers.

One of the first things I wanted to do at the event was to give my thanks to one of the London Marathon Events Company staff. Ellie is her name, but I was told was not at the event today and subsequently found out that her absence was due to attending a wedding this weekend. It was a disappointment being so keen to thank her personally. All I could do was ask her colleagues to pass my message of thanks on when they see her. Whether they do this will remains a doubt. However, I did email her my gratitude when I got back home in Bulgaria.

All was ready to get kitted out into the swimming outfit, namely my wetsuit. I waited until the last possible moment to change in case my stomach had needs. That planned delay was a wise move along with another toilet trip and more movement in my bowels. This now with just 30 minutes before the start of my wave. I knew that there was now a new window of opportunity to go swimming in a wetsuit with a reduced risk of toiletry urges after that.

As usual, it took a while to get the wetsuit in the changing rooms that had murmurs of an exciting atmosphere that rose by the minute. The smell of lubes and heat rubs filled the tent, which added to that sporting atmosphere and heightened the feeling of anticipation. Lubes were a good idea and something I didn't think of or plan with the water temperature at around 16-17C. Having never swum in water less than 26C this was unknown territory for me. I bought a small tin of Vaseline in Sainsbury's yesterday and liberally smeared around the lower part of my neck where the wetsuit collar rubs; I have scars to prove it. All was now ready apart from the final zip fastening at the back which remained un-zipped at this stage.

A kit bag was given to me from the information tent and stuffed up with my clothing and personal belongings. Despite travelling light, there was a fear that all my dressing and personal effects wouldn't fit in. With the volume of clothing I had to cram in, it was severely overloaded. This forcing caused the plastic seals to rip apart at the top. Some improvisation was needed to stop things spilling out. It was a pity I couldn't have used my Asda shopping bag for this; it would have done a better job.

In the 50 metres from the baggage drop off point area to the starting grid, at least five people asked me if I wanted my wetsuit zip done up. It was very disappointing that all these offers to zip me up were from men! When the time was right, I found someone else who also had a zip undone and we reciprocated. He was much taller than me and of Dutch origin. I made a 'pig's ear' of an effort to do up his zip, the reason being it zipped up from top to bottom not bottom to top. I finally got him sealed up after the fifth attempt and just showed up my inexperienced with wetsuits.

Official photographers were swarming the place consistently calling swimmers for shots. It was distinctly disorientating knowing which way to pose with the antiphonal effect of shouting from all angles. We all slowly made our way to the starting point like an ever-increasing flock of multi-coloured penguins funnelling through. What a refreshing sight it was seeing hundreds of swimmers from all walks of life with one goal in mind moving forward together. Our wave had red swim caps and we were the first 2-mile group along with the gold swim capped Super 6-miler folk - respect for these guys man!

Wave Start Times Displayed

It became clear from conversations with others that the main issue with the swim was getting whacked by aggressive elite swimmers. There was an enormous void of understanding why this only happens in the sport of swimming; a supposedly non-contact sport. In cycling and running, if you got to overtake someone you don't ride or run into the back of them, you pass by on the side. Why doesn't it happen in this sport was a question constantly begging to be answered.

There was a cordoned off warm-up area with many venturing into it before diving in for the swim. Warm-up? What a paradox, the water was bloody freezing. They said it was 17C. To me it 17C doesn't sound too cold on paper, my air conditioner set at 17C in my home spills out warm air! But put your body in 17C water and it's positively freezing. Entering the water in a wetsuit did the job, but it was numbingly cold in the non-covered areas on my feet, hands and face. A little bit scary thinking I could be in for around two hours plus in this temperature. I could bear a short sharp cold shower, but these are always short-lived. My brain was telling the cold never feels cold for too long once in water and active.

Multi-Coloured Penguins (In Black and White)

Without glasses, I can't see. With earplugs in, I can't hear. Being blind and deaf affects things. Not being able to see the laid out marker buoys clearly in the distance and not hear other swimmers or staff in the canoes giving advice and instructions were issues. It was like being encapsulated in a bubble with blurred vision and muffled sound coming from the real world outside.

Three, two, one and go! No rush as we waited our turn to jump off the jetty into the cold water in a staggered manner and the final quest had begun. There was only a minute or so of breaststroke made as it was all I could do being surrounded by splashing and mayhem. I just wasn't going anywhere as every swimmer whizzed ahead leaving me for dead as a tail-ender. What the hell, I just ditched the warm-up routine and it was straight into front crawl. It felt a little stiff with the cold initially, but that wore off very quickly with my mind on keeping up with others with my recently acquired front crawl technique.

It wasn't long after I'd set off and just getting into the comfort zone of the second wind that my left leg started stiffening up with cramp. I'd only been swimming for around 10-15 minutes. Surely it was far too early for this kind of problem. I wasn't sure whether it was caused by dehydration, the cold waters or from the tiredness from the extensive walking I did yesterday. The only solution was to just to try and keep my leg moving with exaggerated motions. I had time to stop and massage, but the competitive element in me refused to do this. The cramps came and went throughout the whole swim with the aching never abated. I just put up with it without stopping just as I did in the pool when this happened. It wasn't pleasant, but there is something quite heroic about dealing with these issues and would make the achievement today more special.

Swimming on reaching the second turn, a new wave of elite swimmers with blue-caps caught us up and battered their way through without any due care or attention. It wasn't fairy stories exchanged speaking to others swimmers before we started, but a stark reality. Nervousness kicked in with this invasion of aggressive swimmers. A shortened breaststroke style adopted making the swim harder, but it was less stressful letting them through with my head up out of water. It is a kind of hopelessness in this situation. You can't steer away from them as they come towards you from both sides like attacking sharks. They hit you on the way past without any remorse. I suffered bangs on my legs and mid-rift frequently while waiting for them to pass by. There was no way I could swim through this for fear of being forcibly ducked with a hit. My worse fear had always been inhaling water in my nose or mouth and compounded being close to people, that's when major panic arrives. With earplugs in, I only heard shouting when the canoeist paddled closer towards me bellowing out instructions. He saw I was in a state of panic. The advice blasted out from one of the safety crew was to let the faster swimmers go past. It was more like an order. There were a couple of other red-capped swimmers in the same situation as me, but they didn't seem to be disturbed too much by the chaos that surrounded them. If I had more confidence in the water, perhaps I would have just ploughed on giving as much as I took as if at war.

My greatest fear was now finally realised; swimming with other people close to me, this was by far the biggest test today. Many of these elite swimmers were seemingly possessed and acted like wild animals without manners or due care for other vulnerable swimmers. Their selfishness left a bad taste in your mouth. Not enjoyable at all!

During this time of being attacked from behind anxiety kicked in immediately. This phase of the swim is vivid and something I remember very well, just like I recall the moment I came so close to drowning all those years ago and in London again. With a big swarm of aggressive swimmers jostling me going around a marker buoy, treading water was the only option during this panic-stricken moment. I hated it, there was nowhere to go, no escape route and didn't want to be here anymore. I was verbally cursing and swore at the swimmers that bullied me going past. They thoroughly deserved those insults.

Trying to regroup my thoughts after the crisis was short-lived, it had to be to complete the course. Anxiety gradually subsided facilitated with my self-disciplined focus back with the swim. Now unhindered with space and time to breathe in my own time was a massive relief. I was internally disturbed and holding back my anger for a quite a while afterwards.

One thing I was proud of was the fact at no time throughout the whole swim did I require the aid of the tow float or attempt to ground my feet, (which I couldn't anyway). As long as my head got above water to breathe and it was for the main part, that was enough. Without a wetsuit, there may well have been the urge to grab the tow float, cling to a marker buoy or beckon help from the safety crew canoe in those panic situations. I'll never know.

Knowing the benefits of regularly looking up checking directions, otherwise known as 'sighting', is essential with front crawl as the swim is blind without it. But we all know disrupts rhythm, consistency and technique. The amount of wandering I did without 'sighting' often enough meant that I had done far more than the 2-mile course. Having to deviate and get back on course happened countless times. More training was needed to get the sighting skills more effective without too much interfering affecting technique. It's my fault with lack of practice in the pool, although it is an awkward and challenging skill to master. Perhaps this was the reason I put it off for so long. In my defence, the focus was always just about learning how to swim.

What do you do if you catch someone and hit them accidentally due to lack of sighting anyway? There were many people I passed and accidentally hit feet in front of me apologising each time. That was the least I could do. My tactics on the day to swim pass people was initially to slow down, steer either left or right in preparation, then start speeding up again for the pass. This overtaking method isn't good racing tactics; it was all new to me. This competitive element used was the first time I had an opportunity to pass other swimmers going in the same direction as me. There was a strange logic to being a steamroller swimmer in open water swimming competitions. A beginner's option for approaching a slower swimmer is a simple manoeuvre to avoid contact. Whatever you do to pass with manners will slow you down and impinge on your swimming rhythm and form.

The rest of the swim to the finish was a bit of a blur, but more enjoyable as it went on, albeit being plagued sporadically with bouts of cramp. I do recall front crawl swimming for the vast majority of the swim with intermittent breaststroke during stressful moments with other swimmer traffic. However, this was part of the master plan to counter panic situations anyway. It would have been more than pleasing to manage front crawl throughout like so many others.

The Final Sprint

The final stretch came too soon in my eyes. I wanted to go on and swim more and felt I could have easily coped with another 1-mile lap, even with cramp. I finished with a long sprint over the last 300 metres speeding up right up to the finishing line and overtaking a few other swimmers in the process. There is nothing like being able to produce a competitive element, especially in the final stages of the swim. Racing while swimming was suppressed up until then, with the finishing sprint, it helped ease the pain in my cramped legs strangely enough.

One thing was for sure, even with the consistent cramp I had loads of energy throughout the course and bags more at the end. There was then the thought that perhaps I had over-trained.

Trying to get out of the water at the finish was deceptive. People might look at me and say this guy was utterly exhausted as I collapsed many times while trying to walk up the steep rubber ramp leading out of the water. These tumbles were not from tiredness and fatigue but solely from persistent cramp, causing my legs to seize up. And of course, I was too proud to accept help from the safety staff and the medical team waiting there. Limping towards a photographer, I realised straight away I was being recorded. In an instance, my grimace pose and disabled stance changed from a scene of contortion of pain to a winner's pose and smile for the camera. Somehow the brain controlled the physical issues with the showman striking up another show!

I had to chat with this photographer who told me he will have taken over 2000 pictures by the end of today and loves his job. And what a rewarding vocation he has recording people who are happy setting personal sporting achievements!

A few gingerly steps forward there were lots of young volunteers each with a footstool in front of them. They were waiting to retrieve the timing devices strapped to each swimmer's ankle. All we had to do was raise our leg and place the foot on the stool. The helpers then unstrapped the timer and you are on your way again. As I raised my leg suddenly bout of cramp hit in again and the leg was immediately stepped back down. The only way I could get my foot on that stool was to lie down, roll over on my side with my legs now horizontal with the footstool and then place my foot sideward on the stool. The entertainment was causing a great deal of amusement to all that were watching. The antics were not the showman, but just a practical solution - I think.

Another short walk to the hot tub area after asking for directions. Being as 'blind as a bat' without my glasses on, I couldn't read the direction signs that were on display. This hot tub area reminiscent of a ghost town with eerie phantom-like steam slowly rising from the tubs and drifting silently away. This surprised me as I thought this would be the most popular place heaving with many frozen swimmers in need of warming up.

There was a great sense of liberation after my wetsuit stripped off. To be quite honest, it was only at that moment, it felt like the event had come to an end. There was no hesitation getting in a vacant hot tub albeit gingerly stepping in trying to suppress cramp symptoms. Once in a lovely moment with steam rising like a fluttering curtain in front of me. Through the wall of steam revealed a full view of the Serpentine Lake. A full 10 minutes immersed in warm water warmed-up my body, gradually gave relief from painful cramp issues and now in the knowledge I don't have any more hurdles to get over.

Now out of the hot tub refreshed and warmed up, it was only a short walk finally arriving at the medal presentation area. Six months of training for this moment. As the dangling medals hung and occasionally clanged together around my neck, spontaneous cheering came from the watching crowds now heard clearly without my earplugs in. This brought tears to my eye. One medal was for the 2-mile swim and the other, which was my main goal was 'The London Classics' medal for completing all three London endurance events. And what a beautiful medal that is!

Next was a step up onto a podium with the event sponsor's logo in the background for an official picture. It was a pity the photos taken were with swimmers donning medals after wetsuits had been taken off. Nevertheless, a proud moment with two medals hiding each of my nipples in the shot.

The time given for my swim was 1 hour, 28 minutes and 44 seconds, a time, funnily enough, predicted during training sessions. It was frustrating realising this time wasn't a true reflection of my newly learned swimming ability. The time should have been quicker with more confidence in dealing with other swimmers knocking and battering me. Also, doing this event without any sleep the night before, dehydrated, stomach issues and not least cramp, this would substantially shorten the time. All said and done though I have to be happy with completing the course regardless of time. Earlier in the year, I couldn't swim holding an acute fear of water. Now I stood here victorious after the swim having won the war both mentally and physically.

It was a re-visit to the information desk and thanked the staff for a fantastic day. It then became very emotional and I broke down halfway through my thank you sentence. I had to walk away while they were thanking me for the compliment, which they said made their day.

Talking to strangers and getting onto the subject about why I did the swim was inevitable. The story naturally came out about me learning to swim by myself and not being able to trust others near me in the water. This mistrust comes from thinking panic might occur from others and they will push me under trying to save themselves, which is what happened all those years ago. This fear and anxiety had been with me for most of my life.

More emotions and tears overflowed each time the topic was raised, so I decided not to talk about it anymore from that point.

After pulling myself together, my stomach instructed and me to go and find the toilets again. This urge came unexpectedly, I didn't think I had anything left in my stomach after this morning. Well, when it calls, it calls and I felt much better and certainly less nervous about any toiletry needs for the remainder of the day. I won't have to go through toilet ordeals again after tomorrow when my regular diet kicks back in again.

It was a beautiful day and I wanted to take advantage of the atmosphere for as long as I could. This pining led to me to staying in the park right up until the last swimmer came in at around 17:30. The last swimmer out of the Serpentine Lake completing the event was a middle-aged lady called Helen. She had a massive and loud following from her friends and family. My offer to take a family photo was received with thanks. Naturally, the last swimmer becomes a VIP on-site and in the media and refreshing to see that happen. My vision a couple of months ago was me being in that position.

It was a joy to speak to three strangers who joined me on a free bench on the opposite side of the lake. One of the strangers had Bulgarian parents and that was enough common ground for us to talk for nearly an hour and a half. While talking, we watched the swimmers go by just 20 metres away with a sign of 'No Swimming' in front of us. The other two in conversation with us were a mother and daughter. The daughter had also done the 2-mile swim in a later group with a pink-capped wave. Swimming had helped her get over asthma which was a great story. We tried to get her to contemplate doing all three London Classic events. After seeing my magnificent London Classic Medal, you could see there was a touch of 'I want one' there. It was a pleasure chatting about many things to these people, but not Brexit!

View from the South Side Park Bench

Fish and Chips and beer had always been the plan after leaving the event. I looked at the prices in Hyde Park and they were far too expensive for me to enjoy the meal. With this, I exited the park to hunt a fish and chip shop downtown. It was early evening and my plane was due to leave Stanstead around 12 hours later, so plenty of time to kill. However, I think I made the wrong decision leaving Hyde Park.

After walking for half an hour towards Victoria Coach Station, which is where I had booked a coach to Stanstead at 22:30, there was not one fish and chip shop found during that time. With horrendous traffic, noise and pollution, I'd had enough of this by the time I got to Victoria Station and decided not to hunt for fish and chips anymore. It was Marks and Spencer this time, a former employer of mine. A chicken-based wrap at half-price chosen and bought. Content with that, my evening meal is eaten sitting on a bench in the heart of a busy Victoria Train Station.

Over the next two hours, I didn't move from that bench. I was just reflecting on the day and people watching, a regular and enjoyable hobby of mine. A better plan would have been to stay in the clean and healthy Hyde Park until dusk, then make my way to Victoria Station much later. Too late now.

Victoria Coach Station

It was 20:45 by the time I had taken the short walk to Victoria Coach Station only to discover a coach to Stanstead Airport was due to leave in 10 minutes. Better killing time at Stanstead than hanging around in what felt like an alien London. The coach operator had no issues with me travelling earlier than planned, beside which there were only six people on board by the time we left.

London's Hyde Park was a great place to be and to do this event, but I couldn't wait to get away from London once out of the park surrounds. Looking out of the coach window travelling through the city, I didn't need reminding how happy I was living away from London. Folk say that London is a great place to visit as a tourist, but not to live – I believe that to be true. Even though I am a Londoner, I felt like a foreigner there.

Stanstead airport arrived and it was now the big wait. I had eight hours to kill as I lay on the cold ceramic tiled airport floor in the departure lounge. No time to settle as we were ushered by staff into the arrivals lounge. The departure lounge shut down for a few hours with no flights outbound for the remainder of the night.

I found a new spot to lay down, but the cold ceramic tiles feature on the floor hadn't changed. This time I had company, namely the clickety-click of luggage wheels every few seconds travelling past me across the squared tiles. No chance of sleep, but I had an idea to combat the cold floor. I took my wetsuit out of my Asda bag and lay it on the floor like the sketch of a chalked up murdered person's silhouette. Then I lay on that to give some barrier against the cold tiles. Luckily the wetsuit was almost dry from hanging it out in the park earlier while I was chatting to people. It seemed to do the job, but I couldn't change lying positions without falling out of the silhouette of the wetsuit.

It was a frustratingly long wait. In that time, my medals were taken out and viewed at least three times with causing a great big smile on my face. It was a relief now that this achievement was now history. My thoughts were about getting back home and embrace the new lived freedom away from swimming that awaited me. The stress of swimming sessions, diet restraints and a bombardment of mental labour with the sport can now abstain.

The wait at the airport was on and I wasn't able to sleep. We all witnessed a wedding proposal. This bachelor holding a big bouquet knelt and proposed in front of his girlfriend as she came through the arrival passage. With hundreds of people watching, the girl had a nervous moment of pause before saying, 'Yes'. An unhesitating cuddle and elongated snog sparked off a big round of applause and cheering from the crowds who were enchanted by the scene. This scene was a lovely moment which was in complete contrast from the usual coldness and air of self-importance of travellers in these places.

Should I do the same thing with Galia one day?

Airports are airports and I was soon back on a plane and back home in Bulgaria again. It was a great relief when I finally got back into my car and into an Eastern European timed midday. The drive of 300 kilometres back to my hometown of Yambol had started. No sleep for 48 hours was no problem as I drove on.

I felt a little tired after an hour of driving, so I stopped at a service station for a Bulgarian banitsa and a big cup of strong coffee. The caffeine tricked me into concentrating all the way home and it was a happy man to see Galia again. She had specially prepared a typical Bulgarian meal that evening. My bowels, amongst other things, were amongst the most pleased party that evening!

Why do I get so emotional? There are many factors to this, but the main one is achieving something that I thought was impossible throughout my adult life. The tribulations involved getting a swimming technique that could carry me over that 2-mile finishing line to me was a tremendous personal achievement. It was a nightmare of logistics arrangements getting into the event, tackling the fear of water, dealing with anxiety that is drawn from that and especially swimming close to others. And lastly and not least, everything that surrounded the completion of the challenge was done entirely on my own back.

It was hard to re-adjust once back without a training plan in front of me. For six months, every day, the swim was thought about, and life planned around that. There is now something that surprises me on a day to day basis right now, the fact that I can now swim!

I will wine and dine for a week. Then I can rethink about how I can adjust and chill out now without any immediate sporting challenges in front of me. Is there a hint of doing a Triathlon in the pipeline? There I go again! I will wait for the farm harvest and my wine and rakia made and stored for next year first. There is the winter ahead and lots of time to plan things which we tend to do during the cold spell. I have to admit I'm excited about this. For the first time, I am looking forward to winter so that possible concepts of other challenges explored. But this time hopefully in Bulgaria with some company!

Galia has always been there of course and she has always been very supportive. She is a little proud about this crazy Englishman doing something that is so un-Bulgarian. All the energy, cost and sacrifices made just to get from A-B in some dirty water in London just doesn't make sense to Galia. She was, however thrilled I did it.

Well, the final chapter now closes after jumping over many hurdles on the way to completing the 2-mile open water swim.

As they say, 'The boy did well'

The Awards/Rewards

Medals Awarded

Official Certificate

London Classics Medal Set

Finishing Line Smile

Acknowledgements

Nathan

My youngest son for sorting out billing issues on more than one occasion in the UK

----

realbuzz.com

To RealBuzz.com and some of their valued members.

KickAS_Kate, Libbylaird, Hope_Mountain_Runner and Pandadad

Your encouragement and advice were appreciated!

Ellie

Working at the Helpdesk of London Marathon Events Ltd.

For her undying patience and initiative with my application.

The Mathematics High School, 'Atanas Radev' YAMBOL

To all the staff in the school and the swimming block. Without your help, this challenge and book would not have happened.

Other Books by the Author:

365 Bulgarian Adventures

Written in 2006

Publication Pending

Simple Treasures in Bulgaria

Published 2008

ISBN 978-0-9559-8490-7

Bulgaria's History – A Concise Account

Published 2010

ISBN 978-1-4476-2777-7

100 Essential Recipes from Bulgaria

Published 2011

ISBN 978-1-4477-0260-3